Modern Fiction

General Editor: Robin Gilmour

D0869937

SUSAN DICK

Professor of English Literature, Queen's
University, Kingston, Ontario

Edward Arnold
A division of Hodder & Stoughton
LONDON NEW YORK MELBOURNE AUCKLAND

© 1989 Susan Dick

First published in Great Britain 1989

Distributed in the USA by Routledge, Chapman and Hall, Inc.
29 West 35th Street, New York, NY 10001

British Library Cataloguing in Publication Data

Dick, Susan
   Virginia Woolf. – (Modern fiction)
   I. Title   II. Series
   823'.912

   ISBN 0–7131–6561–8   PBk

Library of Congress Cataloging-in-Publication Data

Dick, Susan
   Virginia Woolf / Susan Dick.
      p.   cm. – (Modern fiction)
   Bibliography: p.
   Includes index.
   ISBN 0–7131–6560–X. — ISBN 0–7131–6561–8 (pbk.)
   1. Woolf, Virginia, 1882–1941 — Criticism and interpretation.
   I. Title.   II. Series.
   PR6045.072Z617   1989
   823'.912—dc 19   88–34069
                                                     CIP

Typeset in 10/12 pt Sabon Compugraphic
by Colset Private Limited, Singapore
Printed and bound in Great Britain for Edward Arnold, the
educational, academic and medical publishing division of Hodder
and Stoughton Limited, 41 Bedford Square, London WC1B 3DQ by
Biddles Ltd, Guilford and King's Lynn

Contents

General Editor's Preface

Fiction constitutes the largest single category of books published each year, and the discussion of fiction is at the heart of the present revolution in literary theory, yet the reader looking for substantial guidance to some of the most interesting prose writers of the twentieth century – especially those who have written in the past 30 or 40 years – is often poorly served. Specialist studies abound, but up-to-date maps of the field are harder to come by. *Modern Fiction* has been designed to supply that lack. It is a new series of authoritative introductory studies of the chief writers and movements in the history of twentieth-century fiction in English. Each volume has been written by an expert in the field and offers a fresh and accessible reading of the writer's work in the light of the best recent scholarship and criticism. Biographical information is provided, consideration of the writer's relationship to the world of their times, and detailed readings of selected texts. The series includes short-story writers as well as novelists, contemporaries as well as the classic moderns and their successors, Commonwealth writers as well as British and American; and there are volumes on themes and groups as well as on individual figures. At a time when twentieth-century fiction is increasingly studied and talked about, *Modern Fiction* provides short, helpful, stimulating introductions designed to encourage fresh thought and further enquiry.

Robin Gilmour

Preface

Virginia Woolf spent her childhood and adolescence in the Victorian age. In the year of her birth, 1882, works by Matthew Arnold, Thomas Carlyle (who had died the previous year), Thomas Hardy, Longfellow, William Morris, 'Ouida', Robert Louis Stevenson, Swinburne, and Walt Whitman were published. 1882 was also the year that would see the deaths of a number of major Victorians, among them Charles Darwin, Emerson, Longfellow, D.G. Rossetti, James Thomson, and Anthony Trollope. The list of works published in 1904, the year that Virginia Woolf (then Virginia Stephen) first published, reflects the transition from one literary age to another which was then underway and in which she would play so significant a part. Hardy is here again, along with Swinburne. But we also find an impressively large assembly of writers whose works would contribute to the evolution of what we now think of as modernism: Joseph Conrad, Ford Madox Hueffer (later Ford), Walter de la Mare, John Galsworthy, George Gissing, W.H. Hudson, Rudyard Kipling, James Joyce,[1] Somerset Maugham, May Sinclair, Arthur Symons, H.G. Wells, W.B. Yeats, and last, but far from least, Sigmund Freud. The major death in 1904, from Woolf's point of view, was that of her father, Sir Leslie Stephen, editor, philosopher, critic, and eminent Victorian. Virginia Stephen grieved for her

---

1 James Joyce, also born in 1882, published his first three *Dubliner* stories in 1904. Later he would set *Ulysses* in this memorable year.

father, but his death freed her, as she later saw, to become a writer.[2] The major transition taking place at the turn of the century in literary history thus coincided with a private one in the life of Virginia Woolf.

Many transitions – historical, literary, and personal – shaped Virginia Woolf's life and career. In the study that follows, I have concentrated on those that reflect her search for ways to express in her fiction her particular vision of reality, a search which led her to experiment with the narrative methods of earlier writers. My concern is in part with those aspects of her fiction which may prove especially challenging to a reader encountering them for the first time: her experiments with narrative voice, with the treatment of character, and with narrative structure. In discussing the development of these aspects of Woolf's narrative method, I draw upon comments she made in her diary, in her letters and in essays, about the writings of her contemporaries and about her own work. These help to establish a context in which her works can fruitfully be read. I also discuss some of Woolf's most important works of short fiction, for she often experimented in these with narrative methods she would develop further in her longer works.

One of the special qualities these related writings draw to our attention is Woolf's interest throughout her career in the part the reader plays in the fiction-making process. 'How Should One Read a Book?', the title of one of her essays, expresses a question she put to herself as she read and wrote about the books of others and as she wrote her own. 'The author would be glad if the following pages were read not as a novel', she noted in the manuscript of her most experimental work, *The Waves*.[3] To read a work of prose fiction 'not as a novel' is, it would seem, to set aside the expectations we ordinarily bring to a novel. Central to these expectations, and to the discussion that follows, is our assumption that a novel will entertain and enlighten us with a story.

Woolf's interest in the act and function of story-telling within the novel began early in her career. Writing in 1905 of a novel called *Rose of Lone Farm*, she complains that the author, Miss Hayden, 'is trammelled by the limitations of the novel form, and is at her best when she describes what she has seen and forgets the necessity of telling a

2 See, for example, her often-quoted diary entry for 28 November 1928: 'Father's birthday. He would have been 96, yes, today; & could have been 96, like other people one has known; but mercifully was not. His life would have entirely ended mine. What would have happened? No writing, no books; – inconceivable' [*D* III 208] (See 'Note on Editions' for a list of abbreviations used in the text and notes.)
3 *The Waves: The Two Holograph Drafts*, ed. J.W. Graham (Toronto: University of Toronto Press, 1976), p. 582 verso.

story' [E I 49]. 'Yes – oh dear yes', Woolf's friend and contemporary E.M. Forster would later write, '– the novel tells a story.' Forster draws a distinction in his study of the novel between 'story', 'a narrative of events arranged in their time-sequence', and the other aspects of the novel – 'people, plots, fantasies, views of the universe' – which convey what he calls 'the life by value', 'that other life' which is more than mere story.[4] Forster's discussion anticipated later theorists who would also distinguish the story (*fabula, histoire, récit*) from what has been variously called *sjuzet, discours,* discourse, and plot. Simply put, in these analyses the story is what happens, while the plot (to use that term) is the 'active interpretive work of discourse on story', the way the story gets told.[5]

Woolf's concern is not only with the way the story gets told, but with the function of the story itself. As her sense of the potentialities of prose fiction develops, her interest in the role the story plays in it becomes increasingly complex. In her 1905 review, she assumes 'the necessity of telling a story' to be responsible for the artificial qualities in *Rose of Lone Farm*. The characters and their actions have been dictated by convention; the vivid details, which are the book's best parts, reflect Miss Hayden's own descriptive powers. In Woolf's first two novels, which I discuss in Chapter 1, she also feels obliged to tell a story and she, too, draws on both the familiar stories and the conventions of story-telling she has inherited from earlier writers. She also begins in these early works, however, to inquire through the thoughts and comments of her characters into the function of story-telling in the individual life. What, for example, do the stories we tell ourselves about our own experiences, and about the people around us, reveal about us, about them, and indeed about life itself?

These large questions become the concern of the narrator of Woolf's third novel, her first extended experimental fiction, *Jacob's Room*. Here Woolf simultaneously uses and challenges the conventions of realist fiction, and in particular of the traditional *Bildungsroman*, a type of novel in which a number of her male contemporaries had already made their mark (one thinks, for example, of E.M. Forster's *The Longest Journey* [1907], D.H. Lawrence's *Sons and Lovers* [1913], and James Joyce's *A Portrait of the Artist as a Young Man* [1916]. Not only does Woolf create a narrator in *Jacob's Room* who

4 E.M. Forster, *Aspects of the Novel and Related Writings*, ed. Oliver Stallybrass (London: Edward Arnold, 1974), pp. 17, 18, and 28.
5 Peter Brooks, *Reading for the Plot: Design and Intention in Narrative* (New York: Vintage Books, 1985), pp. 12–27.

continually draws attention to the challenges she faces as she tries to tell Jacob's story, she also abandons the conventional linear narrative structure she had used in her first two novels (what Joyce once called the 'goahead plot'[6]) in favour of a discontinuous, rhythmical one. Her inquiry into the functions and methods of story-telling, like the demands her work makes on the reader, has now become much more complex.

In the two novels that follow *Jacob's Room*, *Mrs Dalloway* and *To the Lighthouse*, Woolf develops a very different narrative voice, finds a new way to present character, and explores a structure which, while still fragmented, relies far more than that of *Jacob's Room* does on the unifying effects of rhythm. The discoveries Woolf made in writing these novels contributed to her achievement in *The Waves*, which is both her most radical departure from conventional prose fiction and her most profound inquiry into the functions of the story and of story-telling, both in fiction and in the individual life. In the novel that followed *The Waves*, *The Years*, Woolf seemed to many readers to be returning to the nineteenth-century realist tradition she had moved so far away from after her second novel, *Night and Day*. In fact, however, like her more experimental novels, *The Years* is in part an inquiry into the implications of our desire to shape our lives into stories. This inquiry continues in Woolf's last work of fiction, *Between the Acts*, which, as we shall see, asks searching questions and, characteristically, leads us toward only tentative answers about the private stories we tell ourselves and the public ones that we, like the artist, tell one another.

6 James Joyce, *Selected Letters*, ed. Richard Ellmann (New York: The Viking Press, 1975), p. 318.

Note on Editions

References to the novels of Virginia Woolf will be cited within the text. The number given will indicate the chapter, or in the cases of *Mrs Dalloway* and *Between the Acts*, the page, where the quotation is located. The Uniform Edition, published in London by The Hogarth Press, has been used. When needed, the following abbreviations will be given:

BA   *Between the Acts*
JR   *Jacob's Room*
MD   *Mrs Dalloway*
ND   *Night and Day*
TL   *To the Lighthouse*
VO   *The Voyage Out*
W   *The Waves*
Y   *The Years*

References to the short fiction, essays, diaries, and letters of Virginia Woolf will also be cited within the text and identified as follows:

CSF   *The Complete Shorter Fiction of Virginia Woolf*, ed. Susan Dick (London: The Hogarth Press, second edition, 1989).

CEI-IV   Virginia Woolf, *Collected Essays*, ed. Leonard Woolf (London: Chatto & Windus, 1966–7), I–IV.

CRI   (Virginia Woolf, *The Common Reader: First Series*, ed. Andrew McNeillie (London: The Hogarth Press, 1984).

EI-III   *The Essays of Virginia Woolf*, ed. Andrew McNeillie (London: The Hogarth Press, 1986–8), I–III.

DI–V   *The Diary of Virginia Woolf*, ed. Anne Olivier Bell and Andrew McNeillie (London: The Hogarth Press, 1977–84), I–V.

LI–VI   *The Letters of Virginia Woolf*, ed. Nigel Nicolson and Joanne Trautmann (London: The Hogarth Press, 1975–80), I–VI.

1

Traces: Early Fiction

Short Fiction

In 1908, while she was at work on her first novel, *The Voyage Out*, Virginia Woolf declared her intention to 're-form the novel.' 'I think a great deal of my future, and settle what book I am to write', she told Clive Bell on 19 August, 'how I shall re-form the novel and capture multitudes of things at present fugitive, enclose the whole, and shape infinite strange shapes' [*L* I 356]. Less than two years later, In December of 1910, the month and year she would later see as a turning point in modern history, Virginia Woolf told Bell that she had now reached a new stage in her development as a writer. 'I should say that my great change was in the way of courage, or conceit', she wrote, 'and that I had given up adventuring after other people's forms, as I used' [*L* I 446]. By this time Woolf had been publishing essays and reviews for six years. She had also, for a much longer time, been writing short pieces – essays, sketches, short fiction, comic lives – never intended for publication. This was a lengthy apprenticeship and though it had not ended in 1910, for she would continue to write and rewrite *The Voyage Out* for the next two years, it had clearly entered its final phase.

I would like to focus on those aspects of Woolf's early fiction that especially foreshadow the experiments she would undertake later. Throughout her career she often used her short fiction as a testing ground for techniques and themes she would explore further in her longer works. Thus I shall begin by looking briefly at some of the short fiction Woolf wrote in the first decade of the twentieth century, for these works give clear evidence both of the lessons she learned from nineteenth-century fiction and of her growing recognition that her own fiction-making would require her to 'adventure' after 'new forms', not rehearse old ones.

The reader of these early short works is struck immediately by the wide range of narrative techniques Woolf used in writing them. In each she seems to be experimenting with a new method and trying out a new voice. The narrator of what is probably her earliest extant story, 'Phyllis and Rosamond' (1906), presents herself in the opening paragraphs as a social historian who has set out to describe the 'day's work' of two 'daughters at home'. She claims in her stiffly formal introductory comments, as she will again in *Night and Day* (1919), that women who live at home have 'as yet, no title and very little recognition' [*ND* III]. Like Terence Hewet in *The Voyage Out* (1915), the narrator's interest is in what he calls there 'this curious silent unrepresented life' of women [XVI].[1]

Following the essay-like introduction, the narrator presents her central characters, Phyllis and Rosamond Hibbert, daughters of an upper-middle-class family living in Belgravia. She now becomes their invisible companion, a conventional omniscient narrator who overhears their conversations and their thoughts. The day she chronicles is meant to be representative of many: they lunch at home, pay calls with their mother, and attend two parties. The luncheon and party scenes give early evidence of Woolf's sense of the dramatic potential of such social occasions. Her narrator weaves together the party scene and some of the thoughts the scene prompts in the minds of Phyllis and Rosamond. At the second party, which takes place in 'distant and unfashionable' Bloomsbury, Phyllis and Rosamond, like characters who attend some of Woolf's later fictional parties, find their assumptions about themselves disconcertingly challenged. Choosing a suitable husband and then settling comfortably into marriage is not the 'business' of life for the people at this party as it is for Phyllis and Rosamond. Their discovery that some young women have escaped the role of 'slave' [*CSF* 27] is unsettling, but it seems not to change their expectations. Conventional views of romance and marriage, like conventional narrative techniques, will be interrogated more rigorously in Woolf's later fiction.

In a much shorter sketch written during this period, 'The Mysterious

---

1 Woolf revised the paragraph in which Hewet makes this important statement when she prepared the novel for publication in the US in 1920, and this phrase does not appear (see Doran edition, reprinted by Harcourt Brace Jovanovich, p. 215).

Case of Miss V.', Woolf experiments with another way of presenting the lives of two ordinary women. In this sketch the narrator speaks at first, as she does in 'Phyllis and Rosamond', in the voice of a social historian. Her subject is the anonymity and isolation of life in London, a general truth she will illustrate with one of her own experiences. Instead of adopting the stance of an omniscient narrator, however, this narrator now tells her own story in her own voice.

She recounts her search for the mysterious 'Miss V.', a woman she had grown accustomed to greeting at art galleries and concerts but who had, she realized one day, 'ceased to haunt my path' [*CSF* 31]. She makes her way to Miss V.'s flat and discovers there that her shadowy acquaintance has died, apparently (and by an eerie coincidence) at the very moment when the narrator awoke calling her name. While slight, the sketch is an interesting early example of Woolf's sense of the magical potential of names and naming and of her habit of using pairs of sympathetically related characters.

She experimented with first-person narration again in 'The Journal of Mistress Joan Martyn', which she wrote in August 1906, while staying at Blo' Norton Hall in Norfolk. As in the previous stories, Woolf again shapes her narrative around a pair of characters: her first narrator, the historian Rosamond Merridew, and her second, Joan Martyn, the author of the fifteenth-century journal which Rosamond Merridew introduces and which takes up two-thirds of the narrative.

'The Journal of Mistress Joan Martyn' differs from the other two early stories, however, in several important ways. Besides being much longer than these, it also reflects major changes in Woolf's sense of the possibilities of narrative. Rosamond Merridew and Joan Martyn are distinct characters who complement rather than mirror one another. Further, as narrators, they are sharply distinguished from the author, unlike the narrators of the previous two stories. Rosamond Merridew's vigorous, unadorned prose provides an effective preface to Joan Martyn's more varied and frequently poetic style. As an historian, Rosamond Merridew must try to suppress her personality and to imagine past lives; Joan Martyn vividly records her own impressions of the present moment in which she is immersed.

The poetic language of Joan's journal, the dreams and visions, as well as the accounts of the mundane events of her life, make this early work an important prelude to Woolf's later presentations of 'an ordinary mind on an ordinary day' [*CRI* 149]. Also, Woolf's use of the diary format, which enables her to experiment with an elastic narrative that can include anything the narrator wants to record, anticipates

'The Mark on the Wall', 'An Unwritten Novel', *Jacob's Room*, and other later works. This early story also anticipates Woolf's remarkable description, written during a trip to Italy in 1908, of the beauty she hoped to achieve in her writing. After commenting on a fresco by Perugino, she adds:

> As for writing – I want to express beauty too – but beauty (symmetry?) of life and the world, in action. Conflict? – is that it? . . . I attain a different kind of beauty, achieve a symmetry by means of infinite discords, showing all the traces of the mind's passage through the world; achieve in the end, some kind of whole made of shivering fragments; to me this seems the natural process; the flight of the mind.[2]

'The Journal of Mistress Joan Martyn' is the first of Woolf's works to follow the 'traces' of the mind's passage through the world. Joan's thoughts, emotions, and perceptions are presented with the immediacy natural to a diary. Further, the simple chronological structure of the journal allows Woolf to juxtapose reflective passages with others that record events and conversations. These diverse fragments are held loosely together by Joan's distinctive voice. More complex narrative methods for showing 'the flight of the mind' will emerge in Woolf's later fiction as her conviction that 'strong emotion must leave its trace'[3] leads her to explore repeatedly the subtle interaction between present experience and memories, and makes her increasingly aware of the rhythm that informs the mind's processes.

Each of these three works can be seen as an experiment in fictional biography. Woolf imagines particular characters in particular settings and then explores ways of telling their stories. Her persistent interest in the problems a writer faces when she sets out to tell the life-story of another person also animates a fourth early work of short fiction, 'Memoirs of a Novelist' (1909).

This piece can be read from several perspectives: as a commentary on the limitations of a certain type of biography, as a criticism of one kind of Victorian fiction, and as a work of pure fiction itself. Woolf invents three figures: an unnamed reviewer, a biographer, and a novelist. She again uses a pair of characters, for the reviewer speculates about the friendship of Miss Linsett (the biographer) with Miss Willatt (the

2 Quentin Bell, *Virginia Woolf: A Biography* (London: The Hogarth Press, 1972), I, p. 138.
3 'A Sketch of the Past' in *Moments of Being*, ed. Jeanne Schulkind (London: The Hogarth Press, 2nd edn, 1985), p. 67.

novelist), but she also extends this to a triangle as the reviewer herself becomes imaginatively involved in the lives of these two women. She finds that she wants to know more about the inner lives of both Miss Linsett and Miss Willatt than the writings of either woman tell her. She must read between the lines of both Miss Linsett's biography and Miss Willatt's novels in order to discover the relationship between Miss Willatt's life and her works, a relationship she assumes, as Woolf did in her 1909 review of Sterne's biography, the biographer must explore [*E* I 280]. She eventually concludes that in their distance from ordinary life and tiresome moralizing, Miss Willatt's novels reflect the inhibiting egotism of an unhappy and self-centred woman. Similarly, she decides that Miss Linsett's emotional limitations have led her to write a biography that obscures rather than illuminates her friend. In its concern with this failure of feeling, 'Memoirs of a Novelist' anticipates Woolf's later fictional explorations of the barriers that divide one person from another.

Woolf's experiments in these works of short fiction with narrative voice and point of view, narrative structure, ways of presenting characters, and in particular with the representation of the inner lives of women helped to prepare her to undertake the job of 're-forming' the novel, which she would begin in *The Voyage Out*. Although the style of these early pieces lacks the lyricism and rhythmical quality of Woolf's later prose, her use of figurative language, especially in 'The Journal of Mistress Joan Martyn', often foreshadows her distinctive later prose style.

The Voyage Out

In July 1907, Virginia Woolf reflected in a letter to Violet Dickinson on her aspirations as a writer. 'I shall be miserable, or happy', she wrote, 'a wordy sentimental creature, or a writer of such English as shall one day burn the pages' [*L* I 299]. Everything Woolf had written up to this time had been fairly short and had not given her the impetus, or perhaps the challenge, she felt she needed. 'If only my flights were longer', she wrote again to Violet Dickinson later the same month, 'and less variable I should make solid blocks of sentences, carven and wrought from pure marble' [*L* I 300]. *The Voyage Out*, which she probably began to write in the autumn of 1907, would prove to be a much longer 'flight' than any she had attempted before and it would occupy most of her writing energies during the next five years.[4]

Like the early works of most artists, Woolf's first novel shows its debt to the tradition she hoped to challenge. As her title suggests, she makes use of the familiar journey motif in her story. Her central character, Rachel Vinrace, travels from London, where she lives with two elderly aunts, to South America, where she encounters not only a new landscape, but the new emotions of love. The villa where Rachel stays with her aunt and uncle, Helen and Ridley Ambrose, and the hotel where the group of English people on holiday have created their own small community, are drawn together as village households are (for example) in the novels of Jane Austen and George Eliot. Shorter journeys – a picnic up a mountain, a river trip into the interior – and a dance give Woolf the opportunity to develop the relationships between these two groups and in particular that between Rachel and Terence Hewet.

Hewet is the first in a series of artist figures who will appear in Woolf's fiction. His comments on fiction, and in particular his two closely linked desires to learn more about the 'curious silent unrepresented life' of women and to 'write a novel about Silence, . . . the things people don't say' [XVI] draw our attention to the ways that these preoccupations direct the development of *The Voyage Out*. In tracing the changes in Rachel's relationship with the world around her, Woolf attempts to penetrate the inner life of a young woman and to articulate, sometimes in Rachel's voice and sometimes in that of the omniscient narrator, the thoughts and emotions which in ordinary life (and, Woolf believed, in the majority of novels) often remain unexpressed.

Thus she devotes a great deal of time in this long novel to a close scrutiny of Rachel's inner life. At the beginning of the narrative Rachel, who 'had been educated as the majority of well-to-do girls in the last part of the nineteenth century were educated', which means, the narrator explains, that at the age of twenty-four 'there was no subject in the world which she knew accurately' [II], spends much of her time alone reading, playing the piano, or day-dreaming. She sees the people around her as 'symbols', we are told, rather than as complex individuals who are willing to discuss their thoughts and emotions. Rachel has concluded that 'reality' dwells 'in what one saw and felt, but did not

4 For a detailed history of the writing of *The Voyage Out* see Louise A. DeSalvo, *Virginia Woolf's First Voyage: A Novel in the Making* (Totowa, NJ: Rowman and Littlefield, 1980).

talk about' [II]. 'Reality' is a highly charged word in Woolf's vocabulary and it cannot be simply defined. As the verb 'dwell' suggests, reality is a special quality we sometimes perceive in the world around us. For Woolf the word 'reality' encompasses both that quality and our perception of it. She will soon begin to call such moments of intense perception 'moments of vision'; later, she will use the more inclusive term 'moments of being'. As we shall see, many of her subsequent characters will seek ways, as Rachel soon must too, to 'talk about' their perceptions of reality.[5]

This process of articulation is encouraged by Terence. Questioned by him about her life in London, Rachel describes in detail the routine of an ordinary day. She has no difficulty doing this until she reaches the point where she confronts 'the great space of life into which no one had ever penetrated. . . . Hewet was watching her. Did he demand that she should describe that also?' [XVI] His rapt attention tells her that he does and she then describes, probably for the first time, the great pleasure she takes in 'seeing things go on' while remaining herself unseen, unregarded. Her account of the enjoyment she derives from this 'freedom' depresses Terence, for he sees, quite rightly, that she will never commit herself to him as completely as he would like.

Rachel's perception of the 'great space of life' extends the context of her experience by releasing her from what in 'How It Strikes a Contemporary' (1923) Woolf calls 'the cramp and confinement of personality' [*CRI* 238] into a larger, impersonal world. Her presentation in *The Voyage Out* of the moments when characters perceive this enlarged context illustrates her growing sense of such shifts of perspective as part of a general rhythm which shapes 'the flight of the mind'. In the early stories the moments of expanded vision experienced by Phyllis and Rosamond and by Joan Martyn seem to be isolated experiences; in *The Voyage Out* and the novels that follow they become aspects of the patterns of the characters', and the narrators', habits of mind.

Since it will be important to my discussion of the later novels, I would like to take a moment to survey briefly the development of Woolf's awareness of the rhythms of consciousness. In her earliest article on Thomas De Quincey, 'The English Mail Coach' (1906), Woolf describes the expanding and contracting movement of De Quincey's mind and writing in terms that strikingly anticipate her later

5 *Epiphany in the Modern Novel* (London: Peter Owen, 1971) by Morris Beja, which contains a chapter on Woolf, also outlines the history of the concept of the revelatory moment. Woolf offers an eloquent description of 'reality' near the end of *A Room of One's Own* (London: The Hogarth Press, 1974), pp. 165–6.

comments on the function of rhythm in her own writing. 'But if his mind is thus painfully contracted by the action of certain foreign substances upon it', she says after illustrating De Quincey's tendency to digress, 'the conditions in which it dwells habitually allow it to expand to its naturally majestic circumference.' At its best, she adds, De Quincey's writing 'has the effect of rings of sound which . . . widen out and out' to the 'verge of everything where speech melts into silence. . . . beautiful sights and strange emotions created waves of sound in the brain', she imagines, 'before they shaped themselves into articulate words' [E I 367]. The spatial imagery she uses in this early article is echoed in her description in *The Voyage Out* of the way Rachel's mind expands and contracts 'like the mainspring of a clock' when she falls into a state of reverie [X]. The rhymical processes of the mind are associated by such concrete metaphors with the more tangible rhythms of the body.

In the 1920s, Woolf began to reflect in her diary and letters on the function of rhythm in her writing. For example, in November 1924, while she was writing *Mrs Dalloway*, she commented in her diary: 'Thinking it over, I believe its getting the rhythm in writing that matters. Could I get my tomorrow mornings rhythm right – take the skip of my sentence at the right moment – I should reel it off; – . . . its not style exactly – the right words – its a way of levitating the thought out of one –' [D II 322]. These thoughts are echoed in a letter Woolf wrote to Vita Sackville-West while she was at work on *To the Lighthouse*. 'Style is a very simple matter', she asserted, 'it is all rhythm. . . . A sight, an emotion, creates this wave in the mind, long before it makes words to fit it; and in writing (such is my present belief) one has to recapture this, and set this working (which has nothing apparently to do with words) and then, as it breaks and tumbles in the mind, it makes words to fit it' [L III 247].

These insights into the rhythmical impulse that shapes her prose can be linked to a passage in *A Room of One's Own* (1929) in which she comments on the effect the 'wave in the mind' created by a particular scene has on her perceptions. She recalls a scene viewed from her window in which a man and woman approach each other, meet, and enter a cab. She comments: 'The sight was ordinary enough; what was strange was the rhythmical order with which my imagination had invested it. . . . Clearly,' she concludes, 'the mind is always altering its focus, and bringing the world into different perspectives.'[6]

6 *A Room of One's Own*, pp. 145–6.

Woolf's interest in the mind's ability to invest a scene with a 'rhythmical order' is reflected in *The Voyage Out* in the tension that is left unresolved at the end of the novel between disorder and pattern, the seeming randomness of events and the order, and hence meaning, individual characters find in them. Rachel, now engaged to marry Hewet, comes to the conclusion late in the book that the 'strange' haphazard events of her life do in fact form 'themselves into a pattern . . . and in that pattern lay satisfaction and meaning' [XXIV]. Terence, who has probably influenced her in her belief, also assumes that 'there was an order, a pattern which made life reasonable, or, if that word was foolish, made it of deep interest anyhow, for sometimes it seemed possible to understand why things happened as they did' [XXII]. These assumptions will be challenged, however, by Rachel's illness and death. Mrs Thornbury, one of the hotel residents, tries to find solace in the notion that suffering is balanced by happiness, that 'surely order did prevail' [XXVI], but Rachel's death leaves Terence far less sanguine. 'Never again would he feel secure; he would never believe in the stability of life' [XXV]. In her later work, Woolf's exploration of these antithetical perspectives will extend to questions of art as well as of life.

Night and Day

Such an extension begins, in fact, in Woolf's next novel, *Night and Day* (1919), the work she later referred to as her 'exercise in the conventional style' [L IV 231]. Like *The Voyage Out* and her later novel *The Years*, this is a long book, narrated by an omniscient narrator and having a large cast of characters. In it she again draws on the conventions of the love story: Katharine Hilbery agrees to marry William Rodney, but finds herself falling in love with Ralph Denham, who is also loved by Mary Datchet. These pairs and triangles are eventually sorted out when Katharine, who has broken her engagement with Rodney, acknowledges both to herself and to Denham the shift in her affections, and Rodney falls in love with Katharine's lively cousin Cassandra. Only Mary Datchet remains unattached, a single sentry it might seem, left alone at the end overlooking the lives of the others.

The pairings with which the novel ends appears to confirm and extend Katharine's earlier sense of 'some symmetrical pattern, some arrangement of life, which invested, if not herself, at least the others, not only with interest, but with a kind of tragic beauty' [XXIV]. The symmetrical pattern that shapes the lives of the characters, and the plot, is in sharp contrast, however, to the disorder that reigns over Katharine's mother's attempt to write a biography of her famous father, the poet Richard Alardyce. Katharine, who assists her mother in this task, tries to persuade Mrs Hilbery of the necessity of going 'from point to point' [IX], but Mrs Hilbery finds it impossible to transform this morass of memories and manuscripts into a coherent history. As she reviews the opening sections of her mother's draft, Katharine notes with dismay that it soon becomes 'a wild dance of will-o'-the-wisps, without form or continuity, without coherence even, or any attempt to make a narrative' [III]. The challenges that confront the biographer, the need to select and to impose some kind of order on events, and the simultaneous recognition that such an imposed order may falsify life, are, as the narrator of *Jacob's Room* will recognize, those that confront the novelist, too.

These challenges may have contributed to Katharine's sense of the extent to which we shape events into stories in the process of experiencing them and of explaining them to others. When details of her cousin Cyril's irregular life become known, Katharine grows angry at the way her mother and her aunt 'talked and moralized and made up stories to suit their own version' of the situation [IX]. Later, when she is trying to understand her own feelings for Rodney, Katharine tells herself that 'the existence of passion is only a traveller's story brought from the heart of deep forests and told so rarely that wise people doubt whether the story can be true' [XVII]. Ralph Denham expresses a similar sense of the fictive nature of the illusions of love when he tells Mary Datchet that love is ' "only a story one makes up in one's mind about another person, and one knows all the time it isn't true" ' [XIX]. Yet the story he tells himself about Katharine becomes so compelling that when she challenges him with its falsity, he is ready to claim its truth. ' ". . . you go home and invent a story about me, and now you can't separate me from the person you've imagined me to be" ', she tells him, ' "You call that, I suppose, being in love; as a matter of fact it's being in delusion." ' Ralph's response puts the other side of the question: ' "There may be nothing else. Nothing but what we imagine." ' The scene ends with Katharine wondering whether in fact Ralph 'may be looking at something she had never shown to anybody? Was it not something so profound that the notion of his seeing it almost shocked her?' [XXVII]

This scene is one of many in which Woolf explores, as she had in *The Voyage Out* and will again in subsequent works, the difficulties people encounter both when they try to understand their own feelings and when they attempt to understand those of another. Katharine Hilbery has a rich fantasy life into which she retreats periodically, but she reveals this to no one until Ralph Denham presses her to do so. Early in the novel we are told that (like Rachel Vinrace) she was 'inclined to be silent; she shrank from expressing herself even in talk, let alone in writing' [III]. When William Rodney, in an unusual moment of openness, tries to articulate ' "the psychological problem" ', as he stiffly calls it, of ' "romance for a third person" ', Katharine does not tell him that 'her romance . . . was a desire, an echo, a sound; she could drape it in colour, see it in form, hear it in music, but not in words; no, never in words. She sighed, teased by desires so incoherent, so incommunicable' [XXII]. Some time later, however, when Ralph urges her to describe her state of mind, she visualizes it to herself as a scene and then presents this hesitatingly to Ralph. ' "I was thinking about a mountain in the North of England," she attempted. "It's too silly – I won't go on." . . . She could not explain', the narrator adds, 'that she was essentially alone there. "It's not a mountain in the North of England. It's an imagination – a story one tells oneself" ' [XXX]. While a story one tells oneself may not be 'true' as history, as 'an imagination' it is true to the story-teller's inner life.

Katharine tells such stories to herself in order to escape what the narrator calls 'all that part of life which is conspicuously without order'. As the 'daughter at home', Katharine 'had had to consider moods and wishes, degrees of liking or disliking, and their effect upon the destiny of people dear to her; she had been forced to deny herself any contemplation of that other part of life where thought constructs a destiny which is independent of human beings' [XXV]. Like Rachel, and like Phyllis, Rosamond, and Joan Martyn before her, Katharine values the expansive moments when she is able to 'forget herself' [XXVI] in contemplation of a 'vast external world' which is indifferent to human concerns [XXV]. In contrast to her failure to impose a sequential order on the intractable material of Mrs Hilbery's book, she is able to discover, in the rhythms of consciousness, a larger order of which she is a part.

The rhythmical shifts of perspective that shape the processes of the mind are among Woolf's major preoccupations in her first two novels. In both books she seeks ways to describe her characters' perceptions of the world around them and to articulate the things they think and feel but are themselves reluctant or unable to put into words. To a large extent, her methods for presenting character are still those she has inherited from nineteenth-century fiction. Her narrator enters the minds of the characters with ease; she summarizes their thoughts, perceptions, and emotions and quotes the silent discussions they carry on with themselves. Her characters are themselves inquisitive, however, and the questions they ask about human relationships, about the stories they tell themselves and one another, and about the artifices of art prophesy more radical inquiries to come. Like Woolf's early short fiction, these two novels are exploratory. They raise questions about life and the methods of fiction that Woolf will continue to ask in increasingly complex ways.

2

Chasms in the Continuity of
Our Ways: *Jacob's Room*

Essays and Reviews

My discussion of *Night and Day* has taken me into 1919. Before going on to Woolf's third novel, *Jacob's Room*, I would like to shift the chronological perspective for a moment in order to consider some of the essays, reviews, and short fiction Woolf wrote between 1916, the year she resumed publishing essays and reviews (after a two-year hiatus caused by illness), and 1922, the year that *Jacob's Room* was published. This prolific five-year period marks a major turning point in her career. During it she published *Night and Day* and *Monday or Tuesday* (1921), her only collection of short fiction, along with close to 200 essays and reviews in various periodicals. She also wrote several works of short fiction not included in her collection, as well as *Jacob's Room*. I would like first to look briefly at a few of the essays and reviews of this period to see in what ways they reflect the questions Woolf was asking herself at this time about the forms and functions of fiction.

Woolf's steady work as a reviewer (mainly for *The Times Literary Supplement*) kept her in close touch with contemporary writing. For the most part, she reviewed memoirs, biographies, letters, literary studies, and new or newly reissued works of fiction and poetry by British and American writers who ranged from the well-known (such as Henry James, Joseph Conrad, John Galsworthy, and H.G. Wells) to those who were emerging as significant new writers (such as Aldous Huxley, Compton Mackenzie, Edith Sitwell, and Dorothy

Richardson) to those whose works are now generally forgotten (such as Elinor Mordaunt, Thomas Gordon Hake, and Joseph Hergesheimer). Among her most interesting reviews of this period are those of Russian writers, including Chekhov, Dostoevsky, Tolstoy, and Turgenev, whose short stories and novels had begun to appear in English translations.

When Woolf wrote 'Modern Fiction' in 1919 (published originally as 'Modern Novels' in *TLS* on 10 April) and 'The Russian Point of View' in *The Common Reader* (1925), she borrowed a number of passages from her earlier reviews of the short stories of Chekhov and Dostoevsky. These reviews are especially interesting for what they tell us about Woolf's initial response to these 'alien' and 'difficult' writers [*CRI* 180] whose works contrasted so strikingly with those of the English writers Woolf now believed must be improved upon. The questions she asks about their fiction in her early reviews will be partially answered, or at least transformed into conclusions, in her two later essays. The reviews, more than the essays, record the heuristic method which eventually leads her to these tentative conclusions. They present, as she put it in her 1920 review of Chekhov's *The Cherry Orchard*, 'a transcript of individual experience' as she takes the reader through the same process of inquiry she engaged in when she first encountered these writers (*E* III 246).

In 'Tchehov's Questions' (*TLS* 16 May 1918), Woolf reviewed the fifth and sixth volumes of Constance Garnett's translations of Chekhov's stories, along with a translation of his *Nine Humorous Tales*, published in the United States. Although this is her first review of Chekhov's stories, it is clear from her opening comments both that she is already familiar with his work and that she has not yet come to terms with this 'nebulous, undefined' writer. The absence in Chekhov's stories of closed endings surprises her for she 'had been taught', she later says in 'Modern Fiction', that short stories should be brief and conclusive' [*CRI* 153]. At first these inconclusive endings make her feel that 'the solid ground upon which we expected to make a safe landing has been twitched from under us', she writes. But after experiencing this initial giddiness and discomfort, 'we come to feel that the horizon is much wider from this point of view', for she decides, 'we have gained a sense of astonishing freedom.' An expansion of perspective is achieved, then, by a narrative that rejects the comforts of closure. By leaving his questions unanswered, Chekhov suggests that they may in fact be unanswerable. 'Away fly half the conclusions of the world at once', she writes. 'Accept endlessly, scrutinise ceaselessly, and see what will happen.'

While she praises such inconclusiveness for its truth to life and for the way it opens one to experience, Woolf would nevertheless like to come to some conclusions of her own about Chekhov's motives as a writer. 'What was his purpose', she asks in the same review, 'in defining so many scores of men and women, who are for the most part so disagreeable in themselves or in their circumstances so degraded? Did he find no connecting link, no final arrangement which is satisfying and harmonious in itself . . .?' Chekhov can 'split asunder those emotions that we have been wont to think whole and entire', Woolf observes, 'leaving them scattered about in small disconnected splinters. How much of your mental furniture remains entire when you have read 'A Dreary Story'?' This fragmentation of emotions and the absence of a unifying link among them, along with 'an originality in his choice of the elements that make up a story', prompts Woolf to wonder near the end of her review whether Chekhov's 'is not hinting at some other order hitherto unguessed at, though perhaps never fully stated by him' [*E* II 245–7].

The tentativeness of these questions, insights, and opinions is significant, especially when this review is read as the first in a series of commentaries on Chekhov's stories. By the time Woolf wrote 'Modern Novels', and her review of *The Bishop and Other Stories* three months later (*TLS* 14 August 1919), she was far less perplexed by Chekhov's 'inconclusive' stories. 'We are by this time alive to the fact', she wrote in her review, 'that inconclusive stories are legitimate; that is to say, though they leave us feeling melancholy and perhaps uncertain, yet somehow or other they provide a resting point for the mind – a solid object casting its shade of reflection and speculation.' Her metaphors suggest that she may now glimpse the 'other order' in Chekhov's stories, although she can come no closer than this to describing it. She concludes in her review that Chekhov is like the peasant Vassya in 'The Steppe' who, because of his keen eyesight has, Chekhov writes, 'besides the world seen by everyone, another world of his own, accessible to no one else, and probably a very beautiful one' [*E* III 84].

Woolf seems initially to have found the world created in Dostoevsky's fiction both more accessible than that in Chekhov's and more 'bewildering'. When she read a French translation of *Crime and Punishment* in 1912, she declared Dostoevsky to be 'the greatest writer ever born' [*L* II 5]. While reading *The Idiot* in 1915, she compared Scott's characters, 'superb ordinary people', to Dostoevsky's, 'wonders, with very subtle brains, & fearful sufferings' [*D* I 23]. Dostoevsky both surprises and bewilders us, she wrote in 'More Dostoevsky', her.

review of Constance Garnett's translation of *The Eternal Husband, and Other Stories* (*TLS* 22 February 1917), because in reading him 'we find ourselves observing men and women from a different point of view from that to which we are accustomed' [*E* II 86], a point of view that gives us a glimpse of what she calls in 'Modern Fiction' 'the dark places of psychology' [*CRI* 152].

Dostoevsky may well be the first novelist Woolf encountered whose understanding of the rhythms of the mind was consistent with her own. After describing the subtlety with which Dostoevsky traces the mental process that is initiated 'when some startling fact has dropped into the pool of our consciousness', Woolf adds, 'Alone among writers Dostoevsky has the power of reconstructing those most swift and complicated states of mind, of rethinking the whole train of thought in all its speed, now as it flashes into light, now as it lapses into darkness. [*E* II 85]. She would soon demonstrate her own ability at such reconstruction in 'The Mark on the Wall' (1917).

In her review of *The Gambler and Other Stories* (*TLS* 11 October 1917) Woolf again suggests an affinity between herself and Dostoevsky when she describes the way that in the midst of a great medley of voices in 'The Gambler' 'we catch hold of a soliloquy . . . gain in flashes moments of vision such as we are wont to get only from the press of life at its fullest' [*E* II 165]. (She will use this passage in 'The Russian Point of View'.) Her interest in the writer's ability to capture the intense 'states of mind' she now begins to call 'moments of vision' is reflected in several other reviews of this period. In 'Mr Sassoon's Poems' (*TLS* 31 May 1917), 'Lord Jim' (*TLS* 26 July 1917), and in 'Moments of Vision', a review of *Trivia* by Logan Pearsall Smith (*TLS* 23 May 1918), she uses 'moments of vision' to refer to what in the latter review she calls the 'moments which break off from the mass, in which without bidding things come together in a combination of inexplicable significance. . . . Such moments of vision are of an unaccountable nature', she adds. They persist for years in the memory, but 'write them down and they die beneath the pen' [*E* II 250–1]. As we shall see, Woolf will have more faith in the writer's ability to translate at least some remnants of these moments into words by the time she comes to write *Jacob's Room*.

In both 'Modern Fiction' and 'The Russian Point of View' Woolf concentrates on the triumvirate – Chekhov, Dostoevsky, and Tolstoy – and makes no reference to Turgenev, whose works she also read and reviewed during this period. She refers to him briefly in her diary in 1917, and in 1921 she reviewed Constance Garnett's translation of *The Two Friends and Other Stories* (*TLS* 8 December 1921). As in her reviews of the stories of Chekhov and Dostoevsky, she recreates here her initial responses to Turgenev's fiction. After first wondering if he may not be too attentive to details, she decided that the accumulation of vividly rendered scenes brings into the stories 'contrast, distance, solidity', The scenes form a 'succession' and are 'attached to one another by the feelings which are common to humanity'. Turgenev, she concludes, has created 'a world able to exist by itself.' Her praise of his ability to fuse the elements in a scene 'in one moment of great intensity' recalls her comment on the 'moments of vision' Dostoevsky creates in 'The Gambler'. And her discovery in Turgenev's stories of a unity achieved through the exploration of feelings 'common to humanity' echoes her recognition of the 'other order' Chekhov hints at in his stories through his subtle examination of the 'soul' [*E* III 315–17].

A preoccupation with the 'soul' characterizes Russian fiction in general, Woolf later claims in 'The Russian Point of View'. This aspect of their fiction leads her in 'Modern Fiction' to call Chekhov, Dostoevsky, and Tolstoy 'spiritual' writers and to contrast them to the popular 'materialists' H.G. Wells, Arnold Bennett, and John Galsworthy. Joyce's *A Portrait of the Artist as a Young Man* and the seven episodes of *Ulysses* that she had read by April 1919, when 'Modern Novels' was published, convinced her that he was the 'most notable' of 'several young writers' who could also be called 'spiritual'. She qualifies her praise of Joyce's desire to 'record the atoms as they fall upon the mind in the order in which they fall', however, by wondering why his work made her feel 'confined and shut in' a 'bright yet narrow room' rather than being (as Chekhov's inconclusive stories made her feel) 'enlarged and set free' [*CRI* 150–1]. She would continue to worry about this sense of confinement in the novels of both Joyce and Dorothy Richardson, and to see it as a result of their failure to escape, as the Russian writers seemed to have done and as she hoped to do, from 'the damned egotistical self' [*D* II 14].

Although she makes no reference to Dorothy Richardson in 'Modern Fiction', her notes on May Sinclair's review of Dorothy Richardson's novels, which interrupt her reading notes on *Ulysses*,[1] suggest that Richardson was in her mind when she referred in 'Modern Fiction' to 'several young writers' whose work could be distinguished from that of

1 Brenda R. Silver, *Virginia Woolf's Reading Notebooks* (Princeton, NJ: Princeton University Press, 1983), p. 18. These notes are in the Berg Collection of the New York Public Library.

their predecessors. In her review of *The Tunnel* (*TLS* 13 February 1919), Woolf focused on Richardson's method of presenting Miriam Henderson's consciousness. After quoting a passage Woolf comments: 'Here we are thinking, word by word, as Miriam thinks. The method, if triumphant, should make us feel ourselves seated at the centre of another mind, and, according to the artistic gift of the writer, we should perceive in the helter-skelter of flying fragments some unity, significance, or design.' Woolf is seeking here, as she is in the stories of Chekhov and Dostoevsky, a method that will penetrate to 'the reality which underlies these appearances' while it also maintains 'the shapeliness of the old accepted forms.' The superficiality of Miriam Henderson's mind, no matter how finely presented, leaves Woolf wondering (somewhat apologetically) whether the 'old method seems sometimes the more profound and economical of the two' [*E* III 11–12].

Short Fiction

Three works of short fiction that Woolf wrote during this period clearly reflect her engagement in the search for new forms: 'The Mark on the Wall' (1917), 'Kew Gardens' (1919), and 'An Unwritten Novel' (1920). When on 26 January 1920, Woolf recorded in her diary her 'idea of a new form for a new novel', she named these three works as its precursors.

> Suppose one thing should open out of another – as in An Unwritten Novel – only not for 10 pages but 200 or so – doesn't that give the looseness & lightness I want: doesn't that get closer & yet keep form & speed, & enclose everything, everything? My doubt is how far it will ⟨include⟩ enclose the human heart – Am I sufficiently mistress of my dialogue to net it there? For I figure that the approach will be entirely different this time: no scaffolding; scarcely a brick to be seen; all crepuscular, but the heart, the passion, humour, everything as bright as fire in the mist. . . . Whether I'm sufficiently mistress of things – thats the doubt; but conceive mark on the wall, K[ew]. G[ardens]. & unwritten novel taking hands & dancing in unity. [*D* II 13–14]

I shall return to this important entry in a moment, but first I would like to discuss briefly the three pieces that Woolf foresees here 'taking hands and dancing in unity.'

The first of these, 'The Mark on the Wall', was written while Woolf was at work on *Night and Day* and published in *Two Stories*, the first publication of the Hogarth Press. 'I shall never forget the day I wrote

The Mark on the Wall', she later told Ethel Smyth, 'all in a flash, as if flying, after being kept stone breaking for months' [*L* IV 231]. What makes this work so important in Woolf's development is the discovery she made in it of a narrative method that would give her the freedom to trace the vagrant path of 'the flight of the mind'. As we have seen, Woolf explores the rhythmical interchange between different states of mind in some of her earlier characters; in 'The Mark on the Wall', the rhythm of these shifts of perspective shapes the narrative itself.

The narrator begins by recalling a day when she noticed a mark on her wall. She then proceeds to re-enact the thoughts this mysterious mark prompted. Like Rachel Vinrace's, the narrator's mind seems to expand and contract as she explores a wide range of subjects, but returns periodically to the immediate scene and the intrusive mark. This rhythm of expansion and contraction gives the work an internal structure very different from that of the traditional linear plot shaped by a pattern of cause and effect. It both recalls the psychological realism she had admired in Dostoevsky and captures what in writing of Montaigne's essays she later called 'the very pulse and rhythm of the soul' [*CRI* 67].

A similar rhythm informs 'An Unwritten Novel', which Woolf was apparently at work on when she wrote the diary entry quoted above. This work was, she told Ethel Smyth, 'the great discovery'. It 'showed me how I could embody all my deposit of experience in a shape that fitted it. . . . I saw, branching out of the tunnel I made, when I discovered that method of approach, Jacobs Room, Mrs Dalloway etc' [*L* IV 231]. The form of this story resembles that of 'The Mark on the Wall' and another work of this period, 'Sympathy'. A particular object – in this case a woman who sits opposite the narrator in a train – prompts the narrator to develop of series of imaginary scenes which are intended as fragments of this woman's life-story. The narrator's thoughts are again shaped by an expanding and contracting rhythm as she projects a fictive world for 'Minnie Marsh' which she tests periodically against her observations of the actual woman opposite her who is meant to be its subject.

Woolf's would-be novelist engages in a comic struggle with the conventions of realist fiction. For example, as she imagines the household 'Minnie Marsh' is on her way to visit, the narrator feels she must include commercial travellers 'if the story's to go on gathering richness and rotundity, destiny and tragedy, as stories should' [*CSF* 117–18]. Her comment recalls Woolf's observation in 'Modern Fiction' that if the writer were free 'and not a slave, . . . there would be no plot, no comedy, no tragedy, no love interest or catastrophe in the accepted style' [*CRI* 150]. The narrator of 'An Unwritten Novel' assumes she is not free, however. 'Rhododendrons would conceal him utterly', she says of her unwelcome commercial traveller, 'and into the bargain give me my fling of red and white, . . . but rhododendrons in Eastbourne – in December – on the Marshes' table – no, no I dare not; it's all a matter of crusts and cruets, frills and ferns' [*CSF* 118].

The narrator's struggle with the conventions of realist fiction links 'An Unwritten Novel' not only to 'Modern Fiction', but also to various essays and reviews is which Woolf explores the particular problems that women novelists face, some of which will concern the narrator of *Jacob's Room*. In her *TLS* review of Léonie Villard's study of nineteenth-century English women novelists, published in March 1920, three months before the publication of 'An Unwritten Novel', Woolf quotes Bathsheba's complaint in *Far from the Madding Crowd*, ' "I have the feelings of a woman, but I have only the language of men" ', and then adds:

> From that dilemma arise infinite confusions and complications. Energy has been liberated, but into what forms is it to flow? To try the accepted forms, to discard the unfit, to create others which are more fitting, is a task that must be accomplished before there is freedom or achievement. [*E* III 195]

She develops this idea further in *A Room of One's Own* (1929) and in her essay 'Women and Fiction', also published in 1929. A novel is, she writes there, 'a statement about a thousand different objects – human, natural, divine; it is an attempt to relate them to each other.' These objects are held together, she says, by the 'force of the writer's vision' and also by an order 'imposed upon them by convention.' Convention, however, has been established by men and represents assumptions about what is valuable and what is not which are often alien to women. 'Thus when a woman comes to write a novel, she will find that she is perpetually wishing to alter the established values – to make serious what appears insignificant to a man, and trivial what is to him important' [*CE* II 145–6]. This passage echoes both Woolf's complaint in 'Modern Fiction' against the 'materialists' who 'spend immense skill and immense industry making the trivial and the transitory appear the true and enduring' [*CRI* 148] and a comment she made in her diary soon after she had completed *Night and Day*: 'I suppose I lay myself open to the charge of niggling with emotions that don't really matter' [*D* I 259].

When the narrator of 'An Unwritten Novel' finally abandons her attempt to imagine a realistic setting for 'Minnie Marsh' and turns her attention to the elusive soul of her obscure heroine, her perspective begins to resemble that of Chekhov and the other Russian writers whom Woolf admired. 'If we are sick of our own materialism the least considerable of their novelists', she says in 'Modern Fiction' of the Russians, 'has by right of birth a natural reverence of the human spirit' [*CRI* 153]. Further, in this shift of emphasis, and especially in the poetic quality of her prose, the narrator of 'An Unwritten Novel' also prophesies the changes that in 1929 Woolf saw occuring in novels written by women. Women novelists will, she assumes, 'be less absorbed in facts and no longer content to record with astonishing acuteness the minute details which fall under their own observation. They will look . . . to the wider questions which the poet tries to solve – of our destiny and the meaning of life' [*CE* II 147]. In *The Waves*, which she will begin to write in 1929, Woolf will attempt to fulfil this prophesy.

The third of the short works of this earlier period, 'Kew Gardens', is an experiment of a strikingly different sort from 'The Mark on the Wall', which preceded it, and 'An Unwritten Novel', which followed. The richly imagined 'I' of the other two works is abandoned here in favour of an impersonal narrator who cannot be identified as man or woman or as in any way a part of the scene described. In 'The Mark on the Wall' and 'An Unwritten Novel' we accompany the narrator on an excursion into the mind's space; in 'Kew Gardens' the narrator remains firmly fixed in the solid world. The expanding and contracting rhythm that shapes the other two works is enacted here in an almost formulaic juxtaposition of scenes: the narrator's attention shifts like a roving camera between the intricate world of the flower-bed with its resident snail and the succession of couples who pass by.

This juxtaposition of scenes is also a juxtaposition of ways of seeing and it is this aspect of 'Kew Gardens' which most anticipates *Jacob's Room*. In her opening description of the flower-bed, Woolf seems to be experimenting with a kind of pure description, with a representation of the vision Lily Briscoe seeks when she wants 'to get hold of . . . that very jar on the nerves, the thing itself before it has been made anything' [*TL* III 11]. The narrator sees the flowers with what Wallace Stevens has called 'an ignorant eye',[2] for they are described as travellers in a foreign land might describe flowers they have never seen before. This is

2 Wallace Stevens, 'Notes Toward a Supreme Fiction', I, i.

the first sentence of the opening paragraph: 'From the oval-shaped flower-bed there rose perhaps a hundred stalks spreading into heart-shaped or tongue-shaped leaves half way up and unfurling at the tip red or blue or yellow petals marked with spots of colour raised upon the surface; and from the red, blue or yellow gloom of the throat emerged a straight bar, rough with gold dust and slightly clubbed at the end.' The precision with which the shape and colour of the flowers are described and the attention, as the paragraph develops, to the play of light within the bed, have led many readers to relate Woolf's descriptive method here to her interest in post-impressionist painting. Another way that the passage suggests this association is in the highly unusual omission of the flowers' names. Few writers would describe a flower-bed in such detail without naming the flowers. By omitting the names, as a painter must, Woolf asks us to see them without taking the shortcut of envisioning lilies, roses, or rhododendrons. She further avoids placing the flowers in a familiar botanical context by drawing descriptive analogies from the animal world – heart, tongue, throat, veins, flesh – and by seeing the colours in their purest values. Red, blue, and yellow, the primary colours, are supplemented by the earth colours, brown, grey, and green. Readers must imagine for themselves 'the spot of most intricate colour' that stains the brown earth as the summer breeze stirs the petals.

The transition at the end of the opening paragraph from the flower-bed to the people in the garden is made by way of perception: the colour is 'flashed . . . into the eyes of the men and women who walk in Kew Gardens in July.' In describing what these people see, the narrator will enter their minds and adopt their points of view. Thus the objectivity of the opening paragraph contrasts in each of the passages describing the people who pass by to the human habit of seeing one's own thoughts reflected in and giving meaning to the external world. These rhythmical shifts between the narrator's impersonal view of the flower-bed and the characters' self-conscious perceptions and preoccupations anticipate the many shifts of perspective that shape *Jacob's Room*.

Jacob's Room

Woolf places great emphasis in the diary entry quoted earlier on the form of her new novel, and it is this aspect of *Jacob's Room* that I would like to discuss first. Like *The Voyage Out* and *Night and Day*, *Jacob's Room* has some of the formal elements one expects to find in a novel: the narrative is divided into 14 chapters and the story of Jacob's life is presented chronologically. Yet as Woolf foresaw, the form of the novel is determined by a process ('one thing' opening 'out of another') rather than by a chain of events linked by causality (the 'scaffolding' she would do without). Spaces on the page intervene between the numerous scenes into which each chapter is divided and more often than not, the narrator provides no transition from one scene to another. A brief look at the opening pages of the novel can illustrate some of the effects and implications of this method.

The narrative opens *in medias res*: ' "So of course," wrote Betty Flanders, pressing her heels rather deeper in the sand, "there was nothing for it but to leave." ' The narrator does not tell us who Betty Flanders is or indeed what place she has left. The only clue we are given to the cause of her departure is her reflection, 'Accidents were awful things', which comes in the midst of the narrator's presentation in the next paragraph of the scene as Betty Flanders sees it through her tears. 'The entire bay quivered; the lighthouse wobbled; . . . She winked quickly. Accidents were awful things. She winked again. The mast was straight; . . .' Next she is interrupted by her son Archer, who is looking for Jacob, and then she concludes her letter. 'Such were Betty Flanders's letters to Captain Barfoot – many-paged, tear-stained. Scarborough is seven hundred miles from Cornwall: Captain Barfoot is in Scarborough: Seabrook is dead.' The narrator uses this series of unadorned facts (we are not told who Captain Barfoot or Seabrook are and we must assume that Betty Flanders is in Cornwall) as the occasion for a brief excursion to Scarborough, where Mrs Jarvis, the rector's wife, observes Betty Flanders at church and thinks of the loneliness of widows. 'Mrs Flanders had been a widow for these two years', we are told, as the narrator seems to overhear Mrs Jarvis's thoughts. This scene is followed by a single line which brings us back to the beach: ' "Ja–cob! Ja–cob!" Archer shouted.' The cry, which will be heard twice more in this scene and will recur periodically throughout the novel, soon also becomes a *leitmotif* for the narrator's search for a way to tell Jacob's story.

The brief unexplained shift from Cornwall to Scarborough that precedes the cry may for a moment give the reader the impression that Betty Flanders has suddenly returned there. This easy movement in time and space (the scene seems to precede the scene on the beach) characterizes the freedom this narrator enjoys from the restrictions of time and place observed by the narrators of *The Voyage Out* and *Night and Day*. 'One thing' opens 'out of another' on the page as in the mind;

the narrative is fragmented as thoughts are and the mind's rhythms rather than logical transitions relate these fragments to one another.

After Archer calls Jacob for the third time, the narrator comments on his voice: 'The voice had an extraordinary sadness. Pure from all body, pure from all passion, going out into the world, solitary, unanswered, breaking against rocks – so it sounded.' A space intervenes on the page and we are then taken into the mind of the painter Charles Steele (whom we will not meet again in the novel): 'Steele frowned; but was pleased by the effect of the black – it was just *that* note which brought the rest together.' What helps to bring *Jacob's Room* together is the rhythmical movement of the narrator's shifts of perspective such as we see here. Her attention expands outward from Archer's cry to the vast world into which it goes unheeded, then contracts again to the scene on the beach as she narrates Charles Steele's thoughts about his painting. The narrator's expansive perspective is always accompanied by a contracting one.

Besides enacting, as in 'The Mark on the Wall', 'Kew Gardens', and 'An Unwritten Novel', the mind's rhythms, this systaltic movement also contributes to Woolf's exploration in *Jacob's Room* of the context of human life and the forces that shape it. The moments when the narrator's perspective expands beyond the immediate scene to describe (for example) the bare hills of Turkey [III], a solitary man crossing a snowy field [VIII], the ancient broad-backed moors [XI], or the 'exaltation' that sometimes takes us out of ourselves [X], are intrusions of another perspective which testify to the existence of 'chasms in the continuity of our ways', brief revelations of the 'uncharted' potentialities of human experience [VIII]. The inevitable contracting counter-movement brings us back to the familiar everyday world in which the characters are embedded, a world determined in this book by the social conventions that shape Jacob's life and by the forces of history that brings about his death in the First World War.

In addition to encountering in these opening pages the formal characteristics of the book as a whole – the fragmented narrative and the rhythmical shifts of perspective which relate the fragments to one another – the reader is also introduced to the narrator, a woman whose running commentary on life and art and, in particular, on the challenges she faces as she tries to tell Jacob's story, keeps her personality in the foreground of the narrative. Woolf effectively combines in this narrative voice the strong personality of an imaginative first-person narrator (the voice we hear in 'The Mark on the Wall' and 'An Unwritten Novel') with the powers and privileges of an omniscient one. The 'ten years' seniority and a difference of sex' [VIII] that divide her from Jacob and influence her view of him are barriers that as a first-person narrator she cannot remove. Yet she will easily indulge an omniscient narrator's prerogatives when it suits her to do so. 'As for following him back to his rooms, no – that we won't do', she counsels herself in one scene. 'Yet that, of course, is precisely what one does', she adds as she then follows him to his rooms and describes what he does there [VIII]. It 'won't do' for a woman to follow a young man back to his room, but a novelist, who enjoys not only omniscience but (when she so desires) anonymity, is free to go wherever she wants. These continual shifts between a limited perspective and an omniscient one enforce the deliberate fragmentation of the narrative. The reader can never settle comfortably into a story told from a single, consistent point of view.

The narrator of *Jacob's Room* is an avid observer who even complains at one point of being 'choked with observations'. Like Katharine Hilbery confronting her mother's mountain of documents, the narrator knows that 'one has to choose', but like Katharine's mother, she laments the harsh necessity of choice: 'wherever I seat myself', she says, 'I die in exile' [V]. By changing her seat with restless frequency, the narrator is able not only to present a multiplicity of scenes and an extremely large cast of characters, but also to view these from a variety of perspectives. In the opening scene, for example, we see the beach as it looks to Betty Flanders through her distorting tears, to Charles Steele who is trying to transfer his vision of it to his canvas, and to Jacob, who mistakes a large rock for his 'Nanny'. Further, as the narrator's perspective changes, so does her tone of voice, which modulates from that of the 'audible' narrator who calls attention to her presence, to that of the self-effacing narrator who exercises a kind of ventriloquism as she enters her characters' minds and quotes or narrates their thoughts.[3] It is this latter narrative voice that Woolf will soon find most suited to her needs.

The restrictions the narrator encounters as she tries to tell Jacob's story not only illustrate the challenges that face both the biographer and the novelist, they are also aspects of Woolf's exploration of a question which is central to all her works: how does one person know another? Although she allows her narrator access to Jacob's mind, these glimpses of his inner life are infrequent and brief; for the most

3 The term 'audible narrator' comes from Dorrit Cohn, *Transparent Minds: Narrative Modes for Presenting Consciousness in Fiction* (Princeton, NJ: Princeton University Press, 1978), p. 25.

part, she must rely on the impressions she and others have of what they see him do and hear him say.

One scene in which Jacob is observed playfully alludes to 'An Unwritten Novel'. At the opening of Chapter III, Jacob, who is going by train to Cambridge for the first time, enters a car already occupied by Mrs Norman, one of many characters, such as Charles Steele, who make only vivid cameo appearances. In an amusing reversal of the situation in her earlier story, the 'elderly lady sitting opposite' becomes the observer instead of the observed. Unlike the narrator of Woolf's story, however, Mrs Norman, who studies Jacob carefully ('for he didn't notice her'), does not even attempt to sum him up. When her son meets her at the station she starts to ask him about Jacob – ' "Who . . ." said the lady, meeting her son;' – but he has already disappeared into the crowd. The lesson of 'An Unwritten Novel' is flatly stated here by the narrator: 'Nobody sees any one as he is. . . . They see a whole – they see all sorts of things – they see themselves.'

A contrary view to this one is given in a later passage, however. After describing the inability of Jacob's friends to say precisely what they think of him, the narrator concludes:

> It seems then that men and women are equally at fault. It seems that a profound, impartial, and absolutely just opinion of our fellow-creatures is utterly unknown. Either we are men, or we are women. Either we are cold, or we are sentimental. Either we are young, or growing old. In any case life is but a procession of shadows, and God knows why it is that we embrace them so eagerly, and see them depart with such anguish, being shadows. And why, if this and much more than this is true, why are we yet surprised in the window corner by a sudden vision that the young man in the chair is of all things in the world the most real, the most solid, the best known to us – why indeed? For the moment after we know nothing about him.
>
> Such is the manner of our seeing. Such the conditions of our love. [V]

The 'either/or' perspective she presents at the beginning of this passage recalls Mrs Norman's nervous surveillance of Jacob's appearance and the conclusions she deduces from this. In contrast to this cataloguing approach, an example of what the narrator calls elsewhere 'character-mongering' [XII], is the moment of vision the narrator experiences as she looks at 'the young man in the chair'. Although in such moments the young man thus seen is 'the best known to us' and the 'most real', she must admit that even this fleeting vision is incomplete. 'But though all this may very well be true', she says after quoting in the next section what Jacob thinks and says as he talks to Bonamy, 'there remains over something which can never be conveyed to a second person save by Jacob himself.' And since Jacob is a 'silent young man' [IV] who remains an enigma to those who befriend and love him, that something remains unknown.

Like an encounter with one of those 'chasms' that may suddenly interrupt 'the continuity of our ways', the moment of vision comes as a surprise. Both experiences can be linked to the apparent randomness of the progress of Jacob's story. While the narrator's shifts of perspective enact an expanding and contracting rhythm which loosely informs the structure of the book, no pattern emerges in Jacob's life itself. Woolf has not shaped Jacob's life-story, as Joyce does Stephen Dedalus's in *A Portrait of the Artist as a Young Man*, for example, to make one event proleptic of the next. As an artist, Stephen will learn how to control rather than be controlled by this apparently deterministic pattern. For him (as he says in *Ulysses*), 'History is a nightmare' from which he is trying to awake.[4] By contrast, Jacob contemplates the past of ancient Greece and, distrusting newspapers, seems unaware of the forces of history which are about to transform his world. Jacob 'had grown to be a man, and was about to be immersed in things', the narrator says of him while he travels happily in Greece [XII]. Neither she nor Jacob attempts to specify what these future 'things' will be.

References to the war begin to appear in chapter XII and these create an ominous counterpoint to Jacob's episodic story. His surname, Flanders, and his age (he goes up to Cambridge in 1906, we learn at the end of the second chapter) tell us that he is likely to become a character in another story (which Woolf once called a 'preposterous masculine fiction' [*L* II 76]) whose unhappy end we already know. History is a nightmare from which Jacob will not awake. 'We start transparent', the narrator observes, 'and then the cloud thickens. All history backs our pane of glass. To escape is vain' [IV].

Jacob's story and the larger story of the war finally merge in the powerful brief final chapter. ' "He left everything just as it was," Bonamy marvelled. . . . "What did he expect? Did he think he would come back? Bonamy's questions, which shock us with the news of Jacob's death, seem to suggest bitterly that like the men in Whitehall who decree 'that the course of history should shape itself this way or that way' [XIII], Jacob ought to have known that men who go to war may not come back." ' 'With equal nonchalance a dozen young men in

4 James Joyce, *Ulysses* (Harmondsworth: Penguin, 1986), p. 28.

the prime of life descend with composed faces into the depths of the sea; and there impassively (though with perfect mastery of machinery) suffocate uncomplainingly together', the narrator records in a chilling passage [XII]. Bonamy's cry as he looks out the window in the final scene, ' "Jacob! Jacob!" ', recalling as it does the other moments when characters call Jacob's name and receive no answer, challenges the passive acceptance of such orderly death. In addition, his cry, which is framed by a description of the leaves outside which 'suddenly . . . seemed to raise themselves' and then sink down again, is a moving expression of 'uncharted' passion. His expansive cry of grief is quickly counterpointed, however, by Betty Flanders's surprising and mundane question, with which the novel closes: ' "What am I to do with these, Mr Bonamy?" She held out a pair of Jacob's old shoes.'

The inconclusiveness of this ending complements that of Jacob's life. His story is over, but it has not achieved closure: the future that Jacob, like the narrator, has assumed he would have remains undefined potentiality. Nor is his past transformed in the text into memory, which has its own shaping power, either by him or by those who knew him. His monument is an empty room, unanswered letters, and a pair of old shoes. And the historical story in which he has been made to play a part will, readers know, achieve only a ragged, inconclusive ending, despite the attempts of the men in Whitehall to impose order on it and thus to make events conform to their plot.

Contemporary reviewers tended to overlook the historical aspect of *Jacob's Room*, an aspect which reflects Woolf's strong ties to the realist tradition, and to focus instead on the ways that her new novel challenged that tradition. She was criticized for telling no story, for creating no characters, and for giving readers the materials for a novel but not putting these together. 'The little flurries of prose poetry do not make art of this rag-bag of impressions', complained one of the least sympathetic reviewers. Other reviewers, although they wished for a story and fully developed characters, praised the beauty of the writing in *Jacob's Room* and Woolf's ability to 'make us feel', as one reviewer put it, 'what she calls "the ecstasy and hubbub of the soul." '[5] It was this aspect of her book that her friends praised, as well. T.S. Eliot wrote, 'You have freed yourself from any compromise between the traditional novel and your original gift. It seems to me that you have bridged a certain gap that existed between your other novels and the experi-

5 Robin Majumdar and Allen McLaurin, eds., *Virginia Woolf: The Critical Heritage* (London: Routledge & Kegan Paul, 1975), pp. 108, 106.

mental prose of *Monday or Tuesday* and that you have made a remarkable success.'[6]

On the whole, the reviews sounded the notes Woolf had expected. 'If they say this is all a clever experiment', she wrote in her diary on 23 June 1922, four months before the publication of *Jacob's Room*, 'I shall produce Mrs Dalloway in Bond Street as the finished product. . . . If they say, You can't make us care a damn for any of your figures – I shall say, read my criticism them. Now what *will* they say about Jacob? Mad, I suppose: a disconnected rhapsody: I don't know' [*D* II 178–9]. She did not concern herself with complaints of the absence of a story in her novel, for she questioned the obligation placed on a novelist to tell one. But she did worry about the way she had drawn her characters. 'But how far can one convey character without realism?' she asked David Garnett, who had written to tell her he liked *Jacob's Room* [*L* II 571]. And to R.C. Trevelyan, who had offered some criticisms of her book, she wrote: 'Of course, the effort of breaking with strict representation is very unsettling, and many things were not controlled as they should have been. It is true, I expect, that the characters remain shadowy for the most part; but the method was not so much at fault as my ignorance of how to use it psychologically' [*L* II 588]. She elaborated this last comment in a letter to Logan Pearsall Smith. 'Next time I shall stick like a leech to my hero, or heroine', she assured him [*L* VI 501]. As we shall see, the story she was then writing, 'Mrs Dalloway in Bond Street', like the novels that would immediately follow it, *Mrs Dalloway* and *To the Lighthouse*, will show her doing just that.

6 Bell, *Virginia Woolf* II, p. 88.

3

Building it Round One:
Mrs Dalloway

'Mr Bennett and Mrs Brown'

Virginia Woolf would soon find occasion to elaborate her question 'how far can one convey character without realism?' In March 1923 Arnold Bennett published an article which was entitled with another question: 'Is the Novel Decaying?' Central to Bennett's answer was his assertion that the 'foundation of good fiction is character creating, and nothing else.' For an example of the failure of contemporary young novelists to build that foundation, he turned to *Jacob's Room*. It is packed and bursting with originality', he conceded, 'and it is exquisitely written. But the characters do not vitally survive in the mind because the author has been obsessed by details of originality and cleverness.'[1] Bennett's remarks prompted Woolf to interrupt work on *Mrs Dalloway*, which she had begun in October 1922, to write the first version of 'Mr Bennett and Mrs Brown', the essay she later expanded and read to the Heretics at Cambridge in May 1924. 'Mr Bennett and Mrs Brown' is as central to the fiction of this period of Woolf's career as 'Modern Fiction' and her reviews of the Russian writers are to *Jacob's Room* and the short works that anticipated it. The elusive 'life' which in 'Modern Fiction' Woolf advises us to find by examining 'an ordinary mind on an ordinary day' is in 'Mr Bennett and Mrs Brown' firmly located in a character. 'I believe that all novels begin with an old lady in

1 Majumdar, *Critical Heritage*, p. 113.

the corner opposite', she claims as she playfully alludes to 'An Unwritten Novel' [*E* III 425]. How, she now wonders, can she present this old lady, renamed 'Mrs Brown', in her fiction?

The questions Woolf asks as she explores this challenge recall those that vex the narrator of *Jacob's Room.* 'For what, after all, is charac- ter –', Woolf asks in the first version of her essay, 'the way that Mrs Brown, for instance, reacts to her surroundings – when we cease to believe what we are told about her, and begin to search out her real meaning for ourselves?'² She sketches an historical account of the treat- ment of character in which she sees Edwardian novelists (Bennett among them) reacting against their predecesors, the Victorians, by turning their attention from the creation of characters, one of the great triumphs of Victorian fiction, to a detailed presentation and critique of the social context in which the characters live. Woolf's contemporaries, the Georgians, react in turn against the Edwardians whom they see, as Woolf writes in 'Modern Fiction', as 'materialists'. Woolf, Joyce, and other contemporary writers cannot simply look back and imitate the Victorians, for not only did 'human character change', she boldly asserts in the later version of the essay, 'in or about December, 1910', but also Russian fiction has made them see how limited earlier methods of creating character are. 'After reading *Crime and Punishment* and *The Idiot*', she writes in the first version of 'Mr Bennett and Mrs Brown', 'how could any young novelist believe in "characters" as the Victorians had painted them?' Familiar characters in Victorian novels are often known by a 'keyword', such as Mrs Micawber's often repeated line, 'I will never desert Mr Micawber.' 'But what keyword', Woolf asks, 'could be applied to Raskolnikov, Mishkin, Stavrogin, or Alyosha? These are characters without any features at all. We go down into them as we descend into some enor- mous cavern. Lights swing about; we hear the boom of the sea; it is all dark, terrible, and uncharted.'³ It is just this 'uncharted' aspect of character, as we have seen in *Jacob's Room*, which some novelists now wish to express.

Woolf celebrates 'the sound of breaking and falling, crashing and destruction' that she hears around her as the conventions used to create characters in the past are overthrown. For she is confident that after the 'season of failures and fragments' to which, she says, they must now reconcile themselves, writers will find a way to

2 *Op. cit.*, p. 118.
3 *Op. cit.*, pp. 117–18.

reconstruct 'from the ruins and splinters . . . a habitable dwelling-place' for Mrs Brown.[4]

She had already set about that reconstruction in 'Mrs Dalloway in Bond Street', the story she began in the spring of 1922, while she was finishing *Jacob's Room*. A brief discussion of the backgrounds and techniques of this story, which in October 1922 'branched' into *Mrs Dalloway*, should serve as a useful introduction to Woolf's fourth novel.

'Mrs Dalloway in Bond Street'

Virginia Woolf was reading *Ulysses* in book form during the late summer of 1922, while she was writing 'Mrs Dalloway in Bond Street', and it may well have had some influence on her story and on the novel that followed. Her diary confirms the proximity of the two activities. 'I should be reading Ulysses, & fabricating my case for & against', she wrote on 16 August 1922. 'I have read 200 pages so far – not a third; & have been amused, stimulated, charmed interested by the first 2 or 3 chapters – to the end of the Cemetery scene; & then puzzled, bored, irritated, & disillusioned as by a queasy undergraduate scratching his pimples. . . . For my own part I am laboriously dredging my mind for Mrs Dalloway & bringing up light buckets' [*D* II 188–9].

Both her method of dramatizing a character's inner life and her choice of what her character would do while she thinks may owe a debt to Joyce. In her story, as in the opening episodes of *Ulysses*, a character leaves home in the morning and while she walks, thoughts prompted by the immediate scene are mixed with memories and reflections. In both works close attention is paid to place and time: the routes of the characters can be followed on a map and both Bloom and Clarissa hear the chimes of a clock. While Clarissa buys her gloves she thinks about the weary shop-girl just as Bloom muses about the butcher while he buys his breakfast kidney. Retrospective thoughts are balanced by anticipation: Clarissa must prepare for her party, Stephen must break with Mulligan, and Bloom must attend Dignam's funeral.

In 'Modern Fiction', as we have seen, Woolf describes Joyce's method as a desire to 'trace the pattern, however disconnected and incoherent in appearance, which each sight or incident scores upon the consciousness' [*CRI* 150]. She did not follow Joyce in presenting a character's thoughts in a way that would seem to imitate their

4   E III and Majumdar, *Critical Heritage*, p. 119.

'disconnected' structure. Also, unlike Joyce, she generally did not abandon the conventional signals that the narrator uses to let readers know they are overhearing a character's thoughts. The following passages illustrate some of the ways their methods differ.

> A raindrop spat on his hat. He drew back and saw an instant of shower spray dots over the grey flags. Apart. Curious. Like through a colander. I thought it would. My boots were creaking I remember now.[5]

> Omnibuses joined motor cars; motor cars vans; vans taxicabs, taxicabs motor cars – here was an open motor car with a girl, alone. Up till four, her feet tingling, I know, thought Clarissa, for the girl looked washed out, half asleep, in the corner of the car after the dance. [*CSF* 155]

In the passage from *Ulysses*, there is a clear distinction between the narrator's observations, which are presented in complete sentences, and Bloom's, which are recorded in fragments meant to imitate the shorthand of thought. In the passage from Woolf's story, the distinction between the two voices is blurred. The first part of the first sentence, with its rhythmical repetition of nouns, seems to be the narrator's description of what Clarissa sees. The latter part, ' – here was an open car with a girl, alone', shifts the narrative more directly into Clarissa's mind by describing the scene in language that could be hers. In the second sentence, Woolf mixes quoted monologue, which Joyce uses, ('Up till four, her feet tingling, I know') with narrated monologue, as the narrator narrates Clarissa's thoughts rather than quotes them ('for the girl looked washed out'). Her use of the conventional tag, 'thought Clarissa', further reminds us of the narrator's presence.[6]

Woolf's story, like *A Portrait of the Artist as a Young Man* and the opening sections of *Ulysses*, is an example of what Dorrit Cohn calls 'figure-oriented' narration. Although 'the narrator continues to narrate' in such works, Cohn writes, '. . . the audible narrator disappears from the fictional world . . . because a fully developed figural consciousness siphons away the emotional and intellectual energy formerly lodged in the expansive narrator.'[7] In *Jacob's Room*, the narrator does at times enter the characters' minds and quote or narrate their thoughts, emotions, and perceptions, but she never sustains that 'figure-oriented' perspective for more than a sentence or two at a time. In 'Mrs Dalloway in Bond Street', by contrast, the narrator so effectively

5 Joyce, *Ulysses*, p. 75.
6 See Cohn, *Transparent Minds*, chapters two and three, for an extended discussions of quoted and narrated monologue.
7 *Op. cit.*, pp. 25–6.

subdues her own voice that the transitions between her comments and her narration of Clarissa's thoughts are unmarked by any noticeable change of tone. This is the narrative method Woolf would go on to develop further first in *Mrs Dalloway* and then in *To the Lighthouse*.

The stories by Katherine Mansfield that Woolf had read by this time may also have played some part in the development of her method. In 'Prelude', 'Bliss', 'Revelations', and 'The Escape', all of which Woolf had read,[8] Mansfield employs an unobtrusive narrator and she uses a mixture of quoted and narrated monologue to present her characters' inner lives. Also, the opening of the story resembles that of many of Mansfield's which, as Antony Alpers points out, start with a character's thoughts and feelings.[9] Although Woolf disliked many aspects of Mansfield's stories, her skilful self-effacement and her ability to move inside her characters' minds must have made a deep impression upon Woolf.[10]

Virginia Woolf's method in 'Mrs Dalloway in Bond Street' also closely resembles in some important ways Henry James's use in many of his short stories and later novels of a central intelligence, a 'figural consciousness' whose experience is James's subject. While Woolf includes some quoted monologue, she tends, like James, and like Joyce in *A Portrait*, to prefer to employ omniscient narration and narrated monologue to render her characters' thoughts, thus allowing the narrator to maintain direct control over the narration.

Woolf's method is not identical to James's, however. Where she most differs from him and, indeed, most looks back to *Jacob's Room*, is in her use of fragmentation. The passage quoted earlier illustrates the continual shifts of perspective found in the story: we see the external scene that Mrs Dalloway sees, then we overhear the thoughts this prompts, then our attention is again directed to the scene as it preoccupies her once more. Further, unlike James, Woolf enters freely into the minds of other characters when it suits her purpose to do so. 'A charming woman, poised, eager, strangely white-haired for her pink cheeks, so Scrope Purvis, C.B., saw her as he hurried to his office' [*CSF* 152]. Scrope Purvis's thoughts helpfully tell us what Mrs Dalloway looks like

8 Woolf set 'Prelude' in type in 1917. For her comments on 'Bliss' and on Mansfield's two stories 'lately printed in the *Athenaeum*', which I assume to be 'Revelations' and 'The Escape', see her diary entries for 7 August 1918 [*D* I 179] and 2 August 1920 [*D* II 55].

9 Antony Alpers, ed., *The Stories of Katherine Mansfield* (Auckland: Oxford University Press, 1984), p. xxiv.

10 For a fuller discussion of this important relationship, see Joanne Trautmann Banks, 'Virginia Woolf and Katherine Mansfield', in *The English Short Story: 1880–1945. A Critical History*, ed. Joseph M. Flora (Boston: Twayne Publishers, 1985), pp. 57–82.

as she stands thinking on the curb. James seldom allows himself such radical and easy shifts away from his central intelligence.

While less wide-ranging than those in *Jacob's Room*, these shifts of perspective create a similar expanding and contracting rhythm which, along with Mrs Dalloway's progress towards the glove shop, give the narrative its structure. The central event in the narrative – Clarissa's purchase of a pair of gloves – is in itself trivial; the 'story' is the character whom readers assemble out of the fragmentary observations, dialogue, memories, and reflections that make up the narrative. Woolf has found a way to 'stick' to this character with a tenacity that eluded her in *Jacob's Room*.

Mrs Dalloway

Thus in writing 'Mrs Dalloway in Bond Street', Woolf discovered a way to use the 'method' of *Jacob's Room* (as she put it) 'psychologically'. In contrast to her previous novel, however, Woolf employs this method not to enact her narrator's attempt to tell another's story, but rather to explore both the ways her characters engage in the process of self-narration as they tell their own stories to themselves, and the ways these private, silent narratives are affected by the characters' relationships with one another. Thus she returns to the preoccupation with the inner lives of characters that dominates her early fiction, but she returns having found a new method for exploring these lives.

One of the ways Woolf extends in *Mrs Dalloway* the narrative method she uses in her story is by enlarging the temporal context of her characters' reflections. In the story, Mrs Dalloway is preoccupied with the impressions of the moment. The memories these prompt are brief and of secondary importance to her response to the immediate scene. In her novel, however, Woolf's characters undertake repeated excursions into the past. 'But every one remembered', Clarissa thinks as she walks toward Bond Street; 'what she loved was this, here, now, in front of her; the fat lady in the cab' [11]. The continual movement of the characters' thoughts between remembering the past and perceiving 'this, here, now' forms one of the dominant rhythms in the novel.

'It took me a year's groping', Woolf wrote in her diary in November 1923, 'to discover what I call my tunnelling process, by which I tell the past by instalments, as I have need of it' [*D* II 272]. Woolf was undoubtedly helped towards her discovery both by her reading of *Ulysses*, where Joyce uses a similar process to present fragments, or 'instalments', of the pasts of Stephen and Bloom, and by her reading of Proust, whose great monument to the powers of memory, *À la recherche du temps perdu*, she had recently begun to read. But while in the novels of Joyce and Proust memory is a vast storehouse randomly filled with relics of the past, in Woolf's it is a far more selective and decorous museum. After remembering Peter Walsh's saying, 'his eyes, his pocket-knife, his smile, his grumpiness', Clarissa marvels that these are the details she recalls 'when millions of things had utterly vanished' [5].

Through her exploration of memory as both a process and a receptical of the past, Woolf suggests that certain incidents become talismanic, that they play central and repeating roles in the processes of self-narration. The opening scene, for example, in which the freshness of the June morning prompts Clarissa to 'plunge' into memories of such mornings at Bourton, introduces the setting for the cluster of talismanic memories Clarissa will call upon throughout the day. The summer at Bourton when she was 18, loved Sally Seton and chose to marry Richard instead of Peter, was a time of potential which she sometimes juxtaposes to the unspecified failures that followed. 'She had schemed; she had pilfered. She was never wholly admirable', she accuses herself late in the book as she contemplates Septimus Warren Smith's death. 'And once she had walked on the terrace at Bourton', she concludes, as if this segment of the past represents the best of what she might have been [203].

While telling over scenes from the past, Clarissa is evoking an earlier self who functions as a mirror in which she sees both resemblances and contrasts to her present self. The past self is, however, only one of many fragments into which Clarissa feels herself divided. For example, after angrily carrying on a silent argument with Peter, who years ago had called her 'cold, heartless, a prude', she tells herself, 'She would not say of any one in the world now that they were this or were that. She felt very young; at the same time unspeakably aged. She sliced like a knife through everything; at the same time was outside, looking on. . . . she would not say of Peter, she would not say of herself, I am this, I am that' [10–11]. This resistance to the closure of definition, to being cast in the role of a type, like her belief that we survive after death 'like a mist' in the places and people we knew best, extends the boundaries of the self, as memories do, beyond the narrow contingencies of the present moment. Nevertheless, a contrary impulse intrudes into her mind periodically to threaten a loss of this expansive self in the reduction to a single imposed role: 'this being Mrs Dalloway; not even Clarissa any more; this being Mrs Richard Dalloway' [13]. Between such extremes is the self Clarissa composes, for example, as she prepares for her party. 'That was her self', she thinks, 'when some effort, some call on her to be her self, drew the parts together, she alone knew how different, how incompatible and composed so for the world only into one centre, one diamond, one woman who sat in her drawing-room and made a meeting-point' [42].

While the consciously assembled self may be made up, as in these examples, of familiar memories, emotions, and ideas which the character recognizes as facets of a continuous identity, self-narration can also involve imaginative self-creation as when, for instance, Elizabeth Dalloway becomes 'a pirate', 'a rider', 'a pioneer, a stray', as she ventures boldly down the Strand [149–52], or when Peter Walsh imagines himself a 'romantic buccaneer' as he pursues a young woman through the streets. His 'escapade' over, Peter acknowledges that his adventure was 'made up, as one makes up the better part of life, he thought, making oneself up; making her up; creating an exquisite amusement, and something more' [60–1]. The self-consciousness that enables Clarissa, Elizabeth, and Peter to be aware that they are 'assembling' or 'making up' a self gives them a source of stability, as it does Katharine Hilbery, who enjoys similar escapades. By contrast, Septimus Warren Smith cannot distinguish memory from fantasy, reality from dream. (Thus the narrator must fill in much of his background for us, rather than present it through his memories.) He has lost the ability to differentiate fictions, which are, as Frank Kermode points out, 'heuristic and dispensable', from myths, which require belief.[11] From Septimus's point of view, every story he tells himself is true.

Woolf's recognition of the multiple components that contribute to the process of self-narration has led her, as the same recognition led Chekhov, Dostoevsky, Joyce, Lawrence, Ford, Mansfield, and others, to 'split up emotions' in the characters which are then 'woven together' in the narrative as a whole [*CRI* 53]. The 'caves' she dug behind her characters would, she planned, 'connect' in the 'present moment' [*D* II 263]. It is the way Woolf accomplishes this weaving together that I would like to consider next.

'I foresee, to return to The Hours', she wrote in June 1923, 'that this

---

11 Frank Kermode, *The Sense of an Ending* (London: Oxford University Press, 1967), p. 104.

is going to be the devil of a struggle. The design is so queer & so masterful. I'm always having to wrench my substance to fit it' [*D* II 249]. As the earlier title, 'The Hours', indicates, the design is formed in part by the passing of time. The 'leaden circles' of the chimes of Big Ben 'dissolve in the air' throughout the single June day during which the novel takes place. By having various characters count them, Woolf is able to impose a temporal design on her narrative, much as Joyce does in *Ulysses*, and as she had done with the chronology of years rather than hours in *Jacob's Room*. Woolf never abandons the linear, chronological frame in any of her fiction, although she will play with it, as we shall see, in 'Time Passes'. Time is (to borrow an image from *To the Lighthouse*) one of the 'iron girders' that firmly upholds the 'swaying fabric' of her narratives.

The passage of time contributes to the momentum created in the narrative by Clarissa's anticipation of her party and by Septimus's determined movement toward death. This conventional linear plot, which links these two interrelated stories, overlays a deeper structure, which follows a circular pattern and which contributes to the expression of character in the narrative. The metaphor of the diamond, used by Clarissa to describe her 'assembled' self, also describes her place at the centre of the narrative. As the title implies, she is the core and the other characters radiate from her like facets in a diamond. One can also think of her as residing at the centre of a system of ever-widening circles with Peter and Septimus in the circle closest to her, Richard and Elizabeth in the next, Miss Kilman in the next, and so on. The shifts of attention away from Clarissa and then back to her, like the shifts of the characters' thoughts from the present to the past, form an expanding and contracting rhythm in the narrative. The contrast between the linear movement of the plot, which suggests a causal pattern of action, and the radial one, which relies for its development on coincidence and repetition, recalls the distinction Woolf makes in 'Modern Fiction' between life viewed as 'a series of gig lamps symmetrically arranged' and life perceived more accurately as 'a luminous halo'. It is the 'luminous halo', the lighted circle of the characters' inner lives, that she seeks to convey in *Mrs Dalloway*.

In order to emphasize the rhythmical, radial form of the narrative, Woolf has abandoned the conventional narrative unit, the chapter. Spaces sometimes divide scene from scene, as they do in *Jacob's Room*, but not always. As the following outline shows, the separate scenes are, however, grouped into blocks which are related to one another through a subtle process of association. I have identified each scene by referring to the characters(s) central to it; abbreviations are used after the first appearance of each name.

(1) Clarissa Dalloway/Septimus Warren Smith/CD/SWS [5–33]
(2) CD alone, with Peter Walsh [33–54]
(3) PW/SWS/PW/SWS [54–113]
(4) Richard Dalloway at lunch, in the street, at home with CD [113–32]
(5) CD, Elizabeth and Miss Kilman/Miss K and ED/Miss K/ED [132–53]
(6) SWS/PW [153–81]
(7) the party: CD-SWS/CD-PW [181–213]

In the first block, a link between Clarissa and Septimus, who never meet, but whose relationship is central to Woolf's narrative design,[12] is suggested by the recurring shifts from her scenes to his. In the third block, in which Peter Walsh and Septimus are similarly linked, the formal association is supplemented as it is in the first block by other details. For example, Peter, whom we already associate with Clarissa, sits near Rezia and Septimus in the park and casually wonders what the 'awful scene' they are clearly having is about. Since he has just been remembering an awful scene with Clarissa at Bourton, she is again linked by a process of association to Septimus. Further, in the dream of the solitary traveller, which seems to be Peter's dream, the figure of 'womanhood' whom the dreamer imagines dispensing 'with a dark flutter of the leaves, charity, comprehension, absolution', will be echoed in the figure of 'the giant mourner' (Peter conflated in Septimus's mind with his dead friend, Evans) whom Septimus sees in the next scene. The second female figure in the dream, 'the mother whose sons have been killed in the battles of the world', is also associated with Septimus, a victim of 'the deferred effects of shell shock' [201]. Both Septimus and Peter need the comfort these female figures offer. Peter, who has just burst into tears in front of Clarissa, makes his need apparent; Septimus, who 'cannot feel', believes himself beyond the reach of such solace. Indeed, the dreamer's vision of being blown 'to nothingness' and of awaiting 'without fear . . . complete annihilation' is more closely associated with Septimus, who thinks persistently of death, than with Peter, who keeps a tenacious hold on life.

12 In the Introduction which Woolf wrote for the American edition of *Mrs Dalloway*, she said that Septimus was intended to be Mrs Dalloway's 'double' (New York: Modern Library, 1928, p. vi). She told Gerald Brenan that her intention was that 'Septimus and Mrs Dalloway should be entirely dependent upon each other' [*L* III 189].

Peter and Septimus are again related in the sixth block where the transition from the scene of Septimus's death to that of Peter's return to his hotel is made by way of the 'light high bell' of the ambulance summoned by Dr Holmes. 'One of the triumphs of civilisation', Peter notes as he hears it, a comment which can also be read as an ironic reference to Dr Holmes [166]. Clarissa is again brought into this conjunction when Peter then reflects on the effect his morning visit with her has had on him all day. '. . . he had found life like an unknown garden, full of turns and corners, surprising, yes; really it took one's breath away, these moments; there coming to him by the pillar-box beside the British Museum one of them, a moment, in which things came together; this ambulance; and life and death' [167]. Peter's moment of vision reminds us of the 'sudden revelations' [36] both Clarissa and Septimus have had and thus further contributes to the network of associations being woven around them. Rezia is brought into this web, too, for Peter's opening analogy not only recalls Clarissa's memories of the garden at Bourton, but also Rezia's sense, as she drinks something sweet Dr Holmes gives her after Septimus's death, 'that she was opening long windows, stepping out into some garden' [165].

Peter's experience in this passage also illustrates the continual enactment through the characters in the novel of the ideas Woolf explores in it. 'In this book I have almost too many ideas', she noted in June 1923. 'I want to give life & death, sanity & insanity; I want to criticise the social system, & to show it at work, at its most intense' [*D* II 248]. With the exception of the 'Proportion and Conversion' passage [110–12] in which the narrator's anger gets the better of her and she speaks directly to us in her own voice, the ideas that preoccupy Woolf in this novel are explored through the thoughts, speech, and actions of her characters. As it was in *Jacob's Room*, Woolf's method of inquiry in *Mrs Dalloway* is heuristic, a seeking out and testing of meaning rather than an imposition and articulation of fixed theories. The thoughts of Clarissa, Septimus, Peter, Rezia and the other characters whose minds the narrator enters are habitually cast in the interrogative mode.

Questions open rather than close possibilities; answers tend to be provisional, like the characters' assembled selves, and subject to continual revision. For example, when at her party Clarissa withdraws into the 'little room' and attempts to come to an understanding of Septimus's death, she tells herself what she imagines to be the story of his suicide by asking a series of questions: how had he killed himself, why had he done it, had he 'plunged holding his treasure', and finally, was he driven to his death by Sir William Bradshaw: 'might he not then have said (indeed she felt it now), Life is made intolerable; they make life intolerable, men like that?' [202–3]. With each question she asks and the answers she finds, Clarissa draws closer to Septimus, so that by the time she asks the last one in this series, she can imagine that she feels exactly what he must have felt.

Not only does the heuristic process serve Woolf's desire to 'keep the quality of a sketch' in *Mrs Dalloway* [D II 312], but further, questions often create, as in this scene, points of emphasis in the narrative as they mark a new phase or a turn in the character's thoughts. Here, for example, after Clarissa imagines that she knows why Septimus has killed himself, she walks to the window and sees the old lady in the room opposite staring 'straight at her!' 'Could she see her?' she wonders [204]. This question remains unanswered, but in asking it Clarissa puts herself for a moment in her neighbour's place. When she had watched her earlier in the day, the old woman had seemed emblematic of 'the privacy of the soul.' '. . . here was one room; there another', Clarissa had thought, arguing silently against both Miss Kilman and Peter, two people who would 'force the soul' by demanding intimacy. 'Did religion solve that, or love?' she had asked triumphantly [140–1]. She feels no need to ask that question this time, but rather is able as she watches the old woman and thinks about Septimus to celebrate both life and death, as well as the co-existence of separateness and communion.

> The young man had killed himself; but she did not pity him; with the clock striking the hour, one, two, three, she did not pity him, with all this going on. There! the old lady had put out her light! the whole house was dark now with this going on, she repeated, and the words came to her, Fear no more the heat of the sun. . . . She felt somehow very like him – the young man who had killed himself. She felt glad he had done it; thrown it away while they went on living. [204]

The lines from *Cymbeline* which had been in both their minds earlier in the day ('Fear no more the heat of the sun'[13]) come back now to express her acceptance of death as a part of life and to underscore the link between Septimus and Clarissa. When at the end of this passage she goes beyond acceptance to a celebration of Septimus's death, her words recall his cry as he leaps from the window, a cry made in part to the old man who stares up at him: 'I'll give it you!' [164]. Woolf makes frequent and deliberate use of the pronoun 'it' in her fiction. In the last sentence of Clarissa's thoughts quoted above, 'it' shifts from meaning 'killed himself' ('glad he had done it') to meaning 'life' ('thrown it

---

13 William Shakespeare, *Cymbeline*, IV, ii, 258–9.

away'). In Septimus's cry, 'it' remains ambiguous, a reference to life or death, and more likely encompassing both. His cry may allude to Christ's last words, 'It is finished'[14] (which Lily Briscoe also says at the end of *To the Lighthouse*, where 'it' is again open to multiple readings). However we read Septimus's words, they seem to express his own sometime view of himself as 'the Lord who had come to renew society, . . . the scapegoat, the eternal sufferer' [29]. Clarissa now receives his gift in the middle of her own offering to life, her party [134–5], for in contemplating his death she escapes for the moment at least the fear of time that had haunted her throughout the day.

The death of this young man who, as Lady Bradshaw tells Clarissa, 'had been in the army' [201], also brings Clarissa to a fuller vision of her social self. Although 'she could feel nothing for the Albanians, or was it the Armenians? but she loved her roses (didn't that help the Armenians?) [133], as she had thought earlier in the day, she now sees this single death as 'her disaster – her disgrace . . . her punishment. . . . She had wanted success, Lady Bexborough and the rest of it' [203]. In implicating first Sir William Bradshaw, a guest at her party, and now herself in Septimus's death, Clarissa has gone some way towards seeing that her love of roses does little to help the Armenians.

The question Peter asks as the next and final scene begins, ' "but where is Clarissa?" ', emphasizes the rhythm of withdrawal and return – both physical and psychological – enacted in the previous scene. The happiness Clarissa feels as she contemplates the young man's death is like that which led Christians to speak of man's fall as *felix culpa*: it is a happiness that transcends the immediate painful emotions and consequences of the event by seeing it in a far larger context. It is this perspective which may most profoundly illustrate Clarissa's 'sanity'. When she 'assembles' and returns to the party, she adds to her assembled self a new understanding of the human capacity for giving. The questions that Sally Seton and Peter ask as the book ends extend this insight beyond the range of Clarissa's experience. ' "What does the brain matter" ', asks Sally Seton, now Lady Rosseter, ' "compared with the heart?" ' Peter silently answers her with his own series of questions: 'What is this terror? what is this ecstasy? . . . What is it that fills me with extraordinary excitement?' The answer, like the questions, confirms how much Peter owes 'the power of feeling' intensely both now and in memory to Clarissa. 'It is Clarissa, he said. For there she was' [213].

14 John 19:30 (King James Version).

In contrast to *Jacob's Room*, which ends poignantly and appropriately with the absence of the central character, *Mrs Dalloway* concludes with her emphatic presence. Peter's moment of vision here fuses his memory of Clarissa at Bourton 'coming downstairs on the stroke of the hour in white' [56] with his perception of her now as she enters the room, 'not dead', as he had earlier and distressingly imagined her [56], but very much alive. By ending *Mrs Dalloway* with this declaration, Woolf emphasizes the centrality of character in this novel and of the 'tunnelling process' that enabled her to give her characters new independence and depth. Peter's moment of vision also sums up the importance of love, the emotion that enables individuals to confirm both their separateness from and their bonds to one another.

'I found Clarissa in some way tinselly', Woolf recalled soon after she finished the book. 'Then I invented her memories' [*D* III 32]. Some early readers of the book, Lytton Strachey and E.M. Forster among them, felt that Woolf had not yet (as Forster put it) solved 'her problem of rendering character.'[15] While she admitted that 'some distaste' for Clarissa persisted which may have made the character inconsistent, as Strachey said,[16] Woolf herself had no doubts about the method she had found to present her. She would now go on to develop this method further, first in a series of stories and then in *To the Lighthouse*, the novel which contains the famous dinner scene, 'the best thing I ever wrote', Woolf immodestly told Vita Sackville-West, 'the one thing that I think justifies my faults as a writer: This damned "method". Because I don't think one could have reached those particular emotions in any other way' [*D* III 373–4]. The refinements and achievements in *To the Lighthouse* of Woolf's 'damned "method" ' are the concern of the next chapter.

15 Majumdar, *Critical Heritage*, p. 177.
16 *Op. cit.*, p. 168 and *D* III 32.

4

Telling Herself a Story:
To the Lighthouse

Short Fiction

In December 1924 Virginia Woolf was completing two books, *The Common Reader*, a collection of essays (published in April 1925) and *Mrs Dalloway* (published in May). 'Still I am absorbed in "my writing" ', she noted on 21 December, 'putting on a spurt to have Mrs D. copied for L. to read at Rodmell; & then in I dart to deliver the final blows to the Common Reader, & then – then I shall be free. Free at least to write out one or two more stories which have accumulated.' She then reflects on these stories and on her writing in general. 'I am less & less sure that they *are* stories, or what they are. Only I do feel fairly sure that I am grazing as near as I can to my own ideas, & getting a tolerable shape for them. I think there is less wastage. But I have my ups and downs' [*D* II 325]. As we have seen, Woolf had also begun to write short fiction while she was completing both *Night and Day* and *Jacob's Room*. In those cases, the short works anticipated new directions in her writing; her sense of the limitations of what she had achieved in the previous novel prompted the short narrative experiments that in turn became the impetus for the next one. But a different kind of process had begun now. Woolf felt an unprecedented self-confidence as she made the final revisions to both *Mrs Dalloway* and *The Common Reader*. The stories that were 'accumulating' so rapidly testify to an imaginative fertility she seems not to have experienced before, especially during the difficult time when she was about to complete a book.

The period between December 1924 and the spring of 1925 was one of gestation both for these stories and for *To the Lighthouse*, which she first refers to in her diary by name on 14 May, *Mrs Dalloway*'s publication day. 'I'm all on the strain with desire to stop journalism & get on to *To the Lighthouse*', she wrote.

> This is going to be fairly short: to have father's character done complete in it; & mothers; St. Ives; & childhood; & all the usual things I try to put in – life, death &c. But the centre is father's character, sitting in a boat, reciting We perished, each alone, while he crushes a dying mackerel – However, I must refrain. I must write a few little stories first, & let the Lighthouse simmer, adding to it between tea & dinner till it is complete for writing out. [*D* III 18–19]

I shall return in a moment to her reflections here on *To the Lighthouse*, but first it will be useful to look briefly at the 'little stories' which formed, as Woolf foresaw, the 'corridor' leading from *Mrs Dalloway* to her next book.[1]

There are eight of these stories, all set at Mrs Dalloway's party and all centred in the mind of one, or sometimes two, characters. Woolf's comment, 'I am less & less sure that they *are* stories', anticipates the desire she expressed in June of that year to invent a new name for her books to 'supplant "novel" . . . But what?' she wondered, with *To the Lighthouse* in mind. 'Elegy?' [*D* III 34]. Both the short and the long narratives she was writing no longer 'fit', to borrow the clothing metaphor she uses in 'Modern Fiction', the labels conventions would pin on them. These eight stories, which have no conventional plot, grew out of Woolf's interest, already evident in *Mrs Dalloway*, in the many 'states of consciousness' people experience. 'But my present reflection', she wrote in April, 'is that people have any number of states of consciousness: & I should like to investigate the party consciousness, the frock consciousness &c. . . . where people secrete an envelope which connects them & protects them from others. . . . These states are very difficult (obviously I grope for words) but I'm always coming back to it' [*D* III 12–13].

In the stories Woolf again uses narrated and quoted monologue, along with the narrator's own description of the character's thoughts, in order to place her characters' inner dramas in the foreground of the narrative. Central to the process Woolf refers to as the secretion of an 'envelope' is self-narration: the men and women in these stories are

---

1 *To the Lighthouse: The Original Holograph Draft*, ed. Susan Dick (Toronto: University of Toronto Press, 1982), Appendix A: 'Notes for Stories', p. 44.

highly self-conscious characters who tell themselves the stories of their lives as they live them. The present moment is repeatedly juxtaposed with scenes from the past, as talismanic memories again provide characters with a source of stability by testifying to the existence of a familiar and valued self now challenged by the unfamiliar emotions called up by the party.

As in *Mrs Dalloway*, the contrast between the characters as they know themselves and as others know them creates a tension which is central in each story to the progress of the narrative. While Woolf makes some use in *Mrs Dalloway* of the character type, the character whose function it is to represent a particular cliché of human behaviour,[2] she extends the potentialities of that convention in these stories. Thus in dramatizing the interplay between character as type – the perspective taken by other characters in the story – and character as complex individual – the perspective shared by the character, the narrator, and the reader – Woolf creates in these stories a wider range of effects, including especially the comic, than she achieved through that interplay in *Mrs Dalloway*. As we shall see, it is this aspect of the stories in particular that made them the 'corridor' to her next book.

To the Lighthouse

By June 1925 Woolf had completed the first drafts of the eight stories and she had also, as she noted, 'thought out, perhaps too clearly, To the Lighthouse' [*D* III 29]. She still had a major decision to make, however. In the May diary entry I quoted earlier, Woolf had foreseen her 'father's character' at the centre of her book, but in other notes apparently written in the spring, it is the role of Mrs Ramsay (who would be modelled on her mother) which preoccupies her.[3] By July she had begun to 'vacillate between a single & intense character of father; & a far wider slower book' [*D* III 37]. And although she did not know when she began to write the book on 6 August whether it would 'be long or short', she had decided, as she wrote at the end of the outline she also made on that day, that the 'dominating impression' would be of Mrs Ramsay's character.[4]

The discussions Woolf carried on with herself as she planned *To the*

2 Maria DiBattista uses this phrase in her discussion of Septimus Warren Smith's function as a character type. *Virginia Woolf's Major Novels: The Fables of Anon* (New Haven: Yale University Press, 1980), p. 43.
3 *Holograph Draft*, Appendix A, pp. 48–9.
4 *Holograph Draft*, p. 2.

Lighthouse not only give us fascinating glimpses of its gestation, they also make clear the autobiographical basis of it. In deciding to write about her parents and her childhood, Woolf began with a ready-made story: 'father & mother & child in the garden: the death; the sail to the lighthouse', as she succinctly described it [*D* III 36]. Further, not only was her story already told, but its principal characters had already been created. 'People will say I am irreverent', she worried a few days before the book's publication [*D* III 133]. Yet her notes also make it clear that 'father and mother' soon transformed themselves in Woolf's mind into fictional characters, too, as Mr and Mrs Ramsay became part of the rich design of the book as a whole, the design through which Woolf would explore the deeper implications both of her familiar story and of the process that enabled her to tell it.

In contrast to *Mrs Dalloway*, *To the Lighthouse* has a clearly defined, externally imposed structure: it is divided into three named parts, each of which is composed of numbered sections. The triadic structure of the book as a whole supports and supplements the systaltic rhythm which informs the narrative on every level. In 'The Window' Lily's reflections on her painting draw our attention to the way the structure embodies that rhythm. 'It was a question, she remembered, how to connect this mass on the right hand with that on the left', Lily thinks after explaining to Mr Bankes that 'A light here required a shadow there' [I 9]. Woolf has herself joined 'the mass on the right hand with that on the left' with the short 'corridor', as she called it, 'Time Passes'.[5] 'The Window', which covers the afternoon and evening of a single autumn day, moves to slow time; in 'Time Passes', 10 years pass within the space of about 20 pages; time slows again in 'The Lighthouse' as Mr Ramsay, Cam, and James spend the morning sailing to the lighthouse and Lily spends the same hours completing her picture. Time expands, contracts, and then expands again. 'Mind time' [*BA* 13] differs from clock time in *Mrs Dalloway*, too, where the narrative pace is determined in part by the expansion or contraction of the characters' thoughts away from or back to the immediate scene, but that contrast does not inform the design of the narrative as firmly there as it does in *To the Lighthouse*.

'Time Passes' can also be associated with the 'shadow' that Lily sees as a necessary complement to the 'light' in her painting. In the opening scene, James's vivid anticipation of the trip to the lighthouse is expressed in metaphors that anticipate the rhythmical progress of the

5 *Holograph Draft*, Appendix A, p. 48.

book itself. Mrs Ramsay has just told him that they will be able to go
' "if it's fine tomorrow. . . ." To her son these words conveyed an
extraordinary joy,' the narrator says, 'as if it were settled the expedition
were bound to take place, and the wonder to which he had looked
forward, for years and years it seemed, was, after a night's darkness
and a day's sail, within touch.' 'Time Passes' will begin with an extension of the 'night's darkness' that falls at the end of 'The Window' and
will conclude with the dawn that becomes the morning of 'The Lighthouse'. 'The Lighthouse' is, at last, the 'day's sail'.

In many ways the method Woolf uses to present character here is like
that used in *Mrs Dalloway*. Her narrator again moves freely among the
characters, entering their minds and using a subtle blend of narrated
and quoted monologue, supplemented by description, to reveal their
inner lives. Their thoughts about one another are again central to
Woolf's method of characterization. Readers know the characters as
they know themselves and as they are known to one another. Although
she places the characters in the foreground of the narrative and generally blends her voice with theirs, the narrator also maintains an independent point of view, as in *Mrs Dalloway*, which enables her to speak
in her own voice. This is most apparent in 'Time Passes', in which the
narrator suddenly distances herself from the characters to focus her
attention on the forces of ruin and renewal at work on their house.
Their story goes on elsewhere, only to be glimpsed by the reader when
the narrator interrupts her lyrical description of their empty house and
the natural world that invades it to record in a series of bracketed
passages, briefly and without emotion, the distressing events occurring
offstage.

Woolf again makes effective use of allusion in drawing her characters. On the third page of the manuscript she wrote, 'That poetry
should be used in quotations to give the character.' She had done this in
a very limited way in *Mrs Dalloway* where, as we have seen, Clarissa
and Septimus coincidentally recall a line from *Cymbeline* ('Fear no
more the heat o' the sun') and Clarissa remembers having once summed
up her happiness with a line from *Othello* ('If it were now to die, 'twere
now to be most happy').[6] Besides reflecting the state of mind of the
character who recalls them, both lines extend Woolf's treatment of the
theme of death in the novel. She makes far greater use of literary
quotations in this work, however, both to 'give the character' and to
serve the development of particular themes.

6 William Shakespeare, *Othello*, II, i, 187–8.

For example, in 'The Window', while Mrs Ramsay reads James 'The Fisherman and His Wife', one of Grimm's fairy tales, she thinks of it as 'the bass gently accompanying a tune, which now and then ran up unexpectedly into the melody' [I 10]. This scene is given in counterpoint to a succession of scenes in which Mr Ramsay strides up and down the lawn shouting out lines from 'The Charge of the Light Brigade', then stops and silently casts himself in the role of the leader of another doomed expedition, and then, finally, seeing his wife reading to his son, feels he must interrupt her to demand sympathy. Like the figure of the doomed hero whom Mr Ramsay borrows from Tennyson's poem, the conflict of wills in Grimm's story of a woman's greed for wealth and power which results in the loss of all the wishes the enchanted flounder had granted her husband, contributes to the 'melody' of the counterpointed scenes: the interplay of emotional demands made and met by Mrs Ramsay, Mr Ramsay, and James. Quotations function similarly in other scenes. Lines from Charles Elton's poem 'Lurianna Lurilee', quoted at the end of the dinner scene; William Browne's poem 'The Sirens' and Shakespeare's sonnet 98, which Mrs Ramsay reads at the end of 'The Window' while Mr Ramsay reads Scott's novel *The Antiquary*; and lines from Cowper's grim poem 'The Castaway', which Mr Ramsay, now playing the role of the 'desolate man', repeats in the final scenes, all contribute to these characters by extending their context in the literary world of which, from our perspective as readers, they are already a part.

Allusions import untold stories into the narrative which supplement those being told by the narrator as well as by the characters, who habitually enrich self-narration with fictions. Cam, for example, recalls both Elizabeth Dalloway and Katharine Hilbery as she imagines, while they sail towards the lighthouse, that they were 'doing two things at once; they were eating their lunch here in the sun and they were also making for safety in a great storm after a shipwreck. Would the water last? Would the provisions last? she asked herself, telling herself a story but knowing at the same time what was the truth' [III 12]. Cam's adventure story, like the many stories, scenes, symbols, and images the other characters use 'to cool and detach and round off' their feelings 'in a concrete shape' [III 8], contributes to the larger fictive world of the novel, for it elaborates and confirms from another perspective Mr Ramsay's sense of himself as a man bravely facing adversity.

While her narrator's relationship to the characters in Parts I and III closely resembles that in *Mrs Dalloway*, the pattern Woolf makes out of the characters' relationships to one another reflects a development in her sense of the potentialities of this aspect of narrative design. In contrast to *Mrs Dalloway*, where one character is placed at the focal point of the narrative and the others are related to her by a complex network of associations, in *To the Lighthouse* there are three principal characters: Mrs Ramsay, who is, as Woolf predicted, at the centre of Part I, and Mr Ramsay and Lily, who at times, and especially in Part III, usurp her place at centre-stage. The systaltic rhythm embodied in the structure of the narrative is repeated in the inter-relationships among these three.

The opening scene in 'The Window' establishes the domestic roles Mr and Mrs Ramsay will play. Mrs Ramsay's answer to the question James must have asked immediately before the narrative begins, expresses her role as giver of comfort: ' "Yes, of course, if it's fine tomorrow," ' she says. Mr Ramsay's blunt contradiction, ' "But . . . it won't be fine" ', followed in turn by her conciliatory reply, ' "But it may be fine – I expect it will be fine" ', nicely adumbrates both the contrast between their points of view (to which I shall return in a moment) and the rhythm of their relationship. Throughout Part I they separate and come together, both physically and emotionally, until in the final scene of 'The Window' they achieve the wordless reconciliation which brings that rhythm to a point of rest. Mrs Ramsay's sudden death in Part II initiates it again; the trip to the lighthouse in Part III enables Mr Ramsay to heal this breach with another, and perhaps final, reconciliation.

The domestic compromise which enables the moment of understanding to happen at the end of Part I is on another level a compromise between two distinct ways of perceiving the world and others. Mr Ramsay's way is that of the philosopher who believes in 'facts' and who seeks truth through what Keats called consecutive reasoning.[7] If thought is like an alphabet, he tells himself in one of the most amusing scenes in the book, then he has reached Q. 'But after Q? What comes next?' he asks as he tries to imagine Z glimmering (like the geranium with which he decorates his thoughts) 'red in the distance' He is, he tells himself, one of 'the steady goers of superhuman strength who, plodding and persevering, repeat the whole alphabet in order'. The other way of discovering truth, he recognizes with some envy, is that of 'the

---

7 John Keats's letter to Benjamin Bailey, 22 November 1817, in *Letters of John Keats*, ed. Robert Gittings (London: Oxford University Press, 1970), p. 37. Keats's distinction in this letter between 'Men of Genius' and 'Men of Power', like his description of 'negative capability' (*Letters*, p. 43), anticipates the contrasts Woolf draws among Mr Ramsay, Mrs Ramsay, and Lily.

gifted, the inspired who, miraculously, lump all the letters together in one flash – the way of genius' [I 6].

This passage will be in our minds when we soon learn of Mrs Ramsay's ability to feel her self shedding its 'attachments' until she has become simply a 'wedge-shaped core of darkness' whose 'horizon' is 'limitless' and who is able (as Clarissa Dalloway imagined her self doing after death) to become part of the world around her. 'Often she found herself sitting and looking, sitting and looking, with her work in her hands until she became the thing she looked at – that light for example' [I 11]. A few pages before this Lily had explained to Mr Bankes that 'the triangular purple shape' in her picture represents 'Mrs Ramsay reading to James' [I 9]. The echo of Mrs Ramsay's metaphor for her unbounded self in Lily's visual image of her is one of many details that express the deep bond between these two women. Lily's ability as she begins to paint to subdue 'all her impressions as a woman to something much more general' [I 9] resembles Mrs Ramsay's ability to escape the social self that must be always 'netting and separating one thing from another', as she puts it to herself during the dinner scene [I 17]. Lily's memory of Mrs Ramsay saying, 'Life stand still here', leads her in Part III to the recognition that these 'little daily miracles, illuminations, matches struck unexpectedly in the dark', rather than 'the great revelation', are the goal of her quest. 'In the midst of chaos there was shape', she thinks as she discovers that the two 'spheres' of life and art may at times mirror one another, 'this eternal passing and flowing . . . was struck into stability' [III 3]. Thus in contrast to Mr Ramsay, whose quest moves in a linear fashion from point to point, Mrs Ramsay and Lily are both capable of achieving the synthesizing vision of the 'genius', 'one of those globed compacted things', Lily thinks, using one of Woolf's favourite images for a vision of wholeness, 'over which thought lingers, and love plays' [III 11].

The thoughts of all three characters move to the familiar expanding and contracting rhythm of consciousness. They think much less about the past in Part I than the characters in *Mrs Dalloway* do, and much more, as the passages I have just discussed indicate, about the questions prompted by the present scene and by their anticipations of the future. The quest implied in the title of the book is repeated in the internal quests of many of the characters. The questions posed by Mr Ramsay ('But after Q?'), Mrs Ramsay ('But what have I done with my life?'), Mr Bankes ('What does one live for?'), and Lily, whose questions are the most inclusive ('What does it mean then, what can it all mean?' and 'What is the meaning of life?') relate the characters to one another in ways of which they are unaware, while at the same time emphasizing the heuristic nature of the narrative. Further, these questions engage the reader in the characters' search for meaning and enable Woolf to 'make' her reader, to borrow Henry James's special use of this verb,[8] by stressing the importance of the *process* of the search and by suggesting repeatedly that any answers one may find are provisional. Like Lily's visions, they must be 'perpetually remade' [III 7]. A search for 'some absolute good, some crystal of intensity, . . . something alien to the processes of domestic life . . . which would render the possessor secure', as the narrator says in 'Time Passes', is bound, this book suggests, to end in failure [II 6]. The 'processes of domestic life' lie at the heart of Woolf's story, and any meaning found in life must take these processes into account.

This is the discovery to which Lily's effort of 'tunnelling her way into her picture, into the past' brings her [III 5]. The systaltic rhythm of consciousness shapes the process of Lily's inquiry in Part III as her attention continually shifts from her painting and the stories she tells herself of the Ramsays to the sailboat that moves slowly beyond the range of her vision. This rhythm is essential to the act of creation, Woolf suggests, for it enables Lily to sustain the double perspective which, as she discovers, the artist must have. 'One wanted, she thought, dipping her brush deliberately, to be on a level with ordinary experience, to feel simply, that's a chair, that's a table, and yet at the same time, It's a miracle, it's an ecstasy. The problem might be solved after all' [III 11]. The next moment Mrs Ramsay miraculously returns to 'cast her shadow on the step. There she sat', Lily acknowledges, and then turns again towards the now invisible sailboat. 'And Mr Ramsay? She wanted him.'[9]

Lily's role in the narrative is complex. She extends Mrs Ramsay's character by sharing her intuitive powers and her ability to perceive the 'miracle' of life in the ordinary events of every day. In turning towards Mr Ramsay after Mrs Ramsay appears on the step, Lily acknowledges that her vision will not be complete until she has brought him into it as well. The solution to the problem depends upon that synthesis, a

8 'In every novel the work is divided between the writer and the reader; but the writer makes the reader very much as he makes his characters. When he makes him ill, that is, makes him indifferent, he does no work; the writer does all. When he makes him well, that is, makes him interested, then the reader does quite the labour.' From 'The Novels of George Eliot' (1866), quoted in *Theory of Fiction: Henry James*, ed. James E. Miller, Jr. (Lincoln: University of Nebraska Press, 1972), p. 321.
9 I quote here from the revised American edition (published by Harcourt, Brace in 1927), to which Woolf added the 'And'.

synthesis that repeats in the context of art the reconciliation achieved on the level of personal relationships at the end of Part I.

As a visual image, the line Lily draws so deliberately in the centre of her 'blurred' canvas is associated with Mr Ramsay, who is 'lean as a rake' [II 9] and whose quest for truth moves in a linear fashion. The line is also associated with the 'masculine intelligence', which Mrs Ramsay imagined sustaining her 'like iron girders spanning the swaying fabric, upholding the world' [I 17]. Lily had earlier envisaged her painting in similar terms. 'She saw the colour burning on a framework of steel; the light of the butterfly's wing lying upon the arches of a cathedral' [I 9]. Lily's metaphor, like Mrs Ramsay's, suggests the balance of opposites Lily seems to discover as she has her vision. 'To achieve vital harmony', Paul Klee has said, 'the picture must be constructed of parts themselves incomplete brought into harmony at the last stroke.'[10] The line in the centre does not represent Mr Ramsay, or the lighthouse, or any other thing, but is rather the last stroke which brings him and Mrs Ramsay, now gone again from the drawing-room steps, into harmony. The line makes visible the metaphoric 'razor edge of balance' Lily has so persistently sought [III 11].

Besides serving Woolf's interest in exploring modes of perception, Lily functions as an important critic of the role Mrs Ramsay plays for the other characters, that of the beautiful, self-sacrificing wife and mother, the celebrated 'angel in the house'.[11] The tension between Lily's profound and unspoken love for Mrs Ramsay and her recognition of the limitations of Mrs Ramsay's understanding of other people's needs and desires is shown most memorably during the dinner scene when Lily, understanding Mrs Ramsay's silent plea that she 'be nice' to Charles Tansley, toys with the notion of *not* being nice to him. Out of her sympathy for Mrs Ramsay she rejects that 'experiment' and does what angels in the house are expected to do, but she guards her self as she plays this role by remembering her painting. 'Then her eye caught the salt cellar, which she had placed there to remind her, and she remembered that next morning she would move the tree further

10 Quoted by Hanna Segal in 'Art and the inner world', *Times Literary Supplement*, 18 July 1975, pp. 800–1. Woolf told Roger Fry, who had said he was sure there was a symbolic meaning in the arrival at the lighthouse which had escaped him, 'I meant *nothing* by The Lighthouse. One has to have a central line down the middle of the book to hold the design together' [L III 385].

11 Woolf discusses this figure, memorialized in Coventry Patmore's poem of that name, in 'Professions for Women'. See the shortened version in *CE* II 284–9 and the complete text in *Virginia Woolf: 'The Pargiters': The Novel–Essay Portion of 'The Years'*, ed. Mitchell A. Leaska (New York: New York Public Library, 1977), pp. xxvii–xxxxiv.

towards the middle, and her spirits rose so high at the thought of painting tomorrow that she laughed out loud at what Mr Tansley was saying. Let him talk all night if he liked it' [I 17]. Lily repeats this talisman four times during the dinner scene. Her 'work', which Mrs Ramsay assumes will never amount to much, shields her against Charles Tansley's discouraging presence ('Women can't write, women can't paint', she remembers him saying) and gives her an alternative, as she tells herself, to Mrs Ramsay's 'mania for marriage'.

This tension between Lily and Mrs Ramsay also draws our attention to their functions as character types, an aspect of characterization which Woolf uses more extensively in *To the Lighthouse* than she did in *Mrs Dalloway*. Mrs Ramsay, the wife and mother who as an 'angel in the house' perfectly embodies what in *Mrs Dalloway* Peter Walsh calls 'that woman's gift, of making a world of her own wherever she happened to be' [*MD* 84], is a familiar figure in nineteenth-century life and art. Indeed, Henry James's description of Virginia Woolf's mother, Julia Stephen, written soon after her sudden death in 1895, sums up many of the salient features of the type. James remembered her as 'such a perfectly precious force for good that one doesn't know what to make of the economy of things that could do nothing with her . . . but suppress her. She was beautifully beautiful', he added, 'and her beauty and her nature were all active *applied* things, making a great difference for the better for everybody.'[12] He could have been speaking of Mrs Ramsay. The other characters are all affected by what she does for them, by the 'application' as wife, mother, and centre of the home, of her beauty and goodness.

Lily Briscoe, unmarried woman and female artist, an 'odd woman' in both the nineteenth and twentieth centuries, can simultaneously appreciate and resist the power of Mrs Ramsay's type.[13] Mr Ramsay, self-absorbed philosopher and imperious patriarch, expresses a type, too, as do the other adult characters: Charles Tansley, the misogynist working-class student; Minta Doyle, the vivacious young woman who loses books and whose 'glow' casts Lily in the shade; Paul Rayley, a 'booby' whom Mrs Ramsay (and probably the reader, too) prefers to the clever Tansley; William Bankes, the fastidious, kindly scientist; and Augustus Carmichael, the enigmatic 'true poet' who 'crowns the occa-

12 Henry James's letter to Mrs Wister quoted in Leon Edel, *Henry James: The Treacherous Years 1895-1904* (Philadelphia: Lippincott, 1969), p. 153.
13 George Gissing presents sympathetic portraits of 'odd women' and celebrates those who succeed in living independent, and thus unconventional, lives in *The Odd Women* (1893).

sion' at the end of the dinner scene and again at the close of the book. Woolf intended the eight children to be 'undifferentiated'. Their presence was important, she noted, 'to bring out the sense of life in opposition to fate'.[14] While in Parts I and III the youngest son James is differentiated through his close tie to his mother and hatred of his father, in playing this familiar Oedipal role he remains a type. A type is a closed form, a contraction of the self to a figure that is fixed, known, incapable of change; to become more than a type, as some of the characters in both *Mrs Dalloway* and *To the Lighthouse* do through the complexity of their inner lives, is to be seen as open, mysterious, capable of expansion. Mrs Ramsay and Lily achieve that expansion in Part I, as we have seen, and Lily repeats and extends this process in Part III. Mr Ramsay might have achieved it in the final scenes, but he does not, for the narrator withdraws from his mind as the narrative comes to a close, leaving his final vision unnarrated. 'What was it he sought, so fixedly, so intently, so silently?' Cam wonders. 'What do you want?' they both wish to ask as the boat approaches the lighthouse [III 12]. They must guess at the answer, for the 'enclosures of reticence'[15] that restrained Mr and Mrs Ramsay at the end of Part I, restrain them all now.

By leaving those questions unasked and unanswered, Woolf emphasizes the link between Lily's effort to complete her painting and Mr Ramsay's determination to complete the trip to the lighthouse. Lily's journey into the past is like that of an elegist who must question the meaning of Mrs Ramsay's death and seek through memory and imagination a reconciling vision. Cam, James, and Mr Ramsay undertake an actual journey and this becomes the occasion for the children to discover something new and enabling in their relationship to their father. What links both journeys is the power of love. 'Love had a thousand shapes', Lily tells herself, as the 'feeling of completeness' she had experienced while staying with the Ramsays 10 years ago returns [III 11]. Cam, helped by memories of her mother, realizes her love for her father more easily than James does, for he must relive and then transcend the hatred he has felt for him since childhood. Two of the closely related images James uses to 'round off' his feelings 'in a concrete shape' vividly express the ambivalence which makes this change of heart so difficult. One, a foot crushed by a wheel, expresses his sense of Mr Ramsay's destructive power, but the other, the scene of footprints in the snow, acknowledges his recognition of the deep bond

14 *Holograph Draft*, p. 3.
15 Joyce, *Ulysses*, p. 558.

between them: there 'were two pairs of footprints only; his own and his father's. They alone knew each other. What then was this terror,' he still must ask himself, 'this hatred?' James is able to put aside that question, for seeing the lighthouse close-up for the first time, he suddenly realizes the effect of perspective: 'So that was the Lighthouse, was it? No, the other was also the Lighthouse. For nothing was simply one thing. The other Lighthouse was true too' [III 8].[16] His father is both the tyrant he hates and the lonely, needful man, the 'castaway', whom he loves.

James's recognition that 'nothing was simply one thing' echoes Cam's ability to tell herself a story while at the same time knowing 'what was the truth', and complements Lily's understanding that 'the vision must be perpetually remade'. The completion of the painting, like the arrival at the lighthouse, is a moment of stability that marks the boundary of the story's action; the process the characters have engaged in does not end, however. Thus although the ending seems closed, it is in fact open, as Lily's use of Christ's last worlds on the cross – 'It is finished' – suggests. The statement was true of Christ's earthly life, but not of His divine one. The rhythm of eternal renewal, 'the incessant rise and fall and fall and rise again' which Bernard will affirm at the end of *The Waves*, is felt, too, at the end of *To the Lighthouse*.

Augustus Carmichael comes forward at the end, 'looking like an old pagan god' to 'crown' the occasion. Lily has felt that he knew what she was thinking as she struggled with her painting and his words and gestures now seem confirmation of this silent understanding. 'But this was one way of knowing people', Lily had thought earlier as she recalled that Mr Carmichael, whose poetry she has not read, is now a famous man, 'to know the outline, not the detail' [III 11]. This is the way the reader knows him, too, for he is the one adult character in the narrative whose mind is, except for one brief moment at the end of Part II, consistently closed to us.

Augustus Carmichael can be taken as a sign of a change coming in Woolf's treatment of character. As we have seen, the narrator of *Jacob's Room* is convinced that 'Nobody sees any one as he is' [III], but the characters in Woolf's next two novels have seemed to challenge that view. Although they make many superficial judgments of others and often see one another as types, they are capable on occasion of seeing facets of another's deeper self. This change within the fiction

16 I have again quoted the revised American edition. The final sentence reads in the English edition, 'The other was the Lighthouse too.'

accompanies the change in Woolf's treatment of character; the inner lives so hard to glimpse in *Jacob's Room* become her preoccupation in the two novels that follow. Lily's acceptance of a knowledge which is limited to the 'outline' of another person reflects Woolf's recognition, apparent in her method of creating characters, of the truth that can be revealed in appearances. The 'apparition' is one part of the self. Augustus Carmichael, who is all apparition, foreshadows the change of perspective which will lead Woolf to a radical reconception of character in *The Waves*, the book in which she 'meant to have' no characters [*D*IV 47]. This change of perspective and its expression in *The Waves* is the concern of the next chapter.

5

Writing to a Rhythm:
The Waves

From *To the Lighthouse* to *The Waves*

Two weeks after completing the first draft of *To the Lighthouse*, Virginia Woolf commented in her diary on the 'intense depression' that had recently overtaken her. 'These 9 weeks give one a plunge into deep waters; which is a little alarming, but full of interest', she noted on 28 September 1926. 'All the rest of the year, one's . . . curbing & controlling this odd immeasurable soul. When it expands, though one is frightened & bored & gloomy, . . . One goes down into the well & nothing protects one from the assault of truth.' Two days later, she added some further remarks to what she called 'the mystical side of this solitude':

> how it is not oneself but something in the universe that one's left with. It is this that is frightening & exciting in the midst of my profound gloom, depression, boredom whatever it is: One sees a fin passing far out. What image can I reach to convey what I mean? Really there is none I think. The interesting thing is that in all my feeling & thinking I have never come up against this before. Life is, soberly & accurately, the oddest affair; has in it the essence of reality. I used to feel this as a child – couldn't step across a puddle once I remember, for thinking, how strange – what am I? &c. But by writing I dont reach anything. All I mean to make is a note of a curious state of mind. I hazard the guess that it may be the impulse behind another book.

Three years later she wrote in the margin beside this entry, 'Perhaps The Waves or moths', thus confirming her guess [*D* III 112–13]. I quote this lengthy passage because it succinctly expresses the 'impulse' behind *The Waves*. This book would have a longer gestation period than any she had yet written and, as this entry indicates, it would explore more profoundly than had any of her earlier works those moments of vision, or as she now sometimes called them, 'moments of being', which reveal the 'essence of reality'.

During the interval between the completion of *To the Lighthouse* and July 1929, when she began the first draft of *The Waves*, Woolf wrote *Orlando* (1928), *A Room of One's Own* (1929), several short stories, and, as always, numerous essays and reviews. The first of the stories, 'Moments of Being: "Slater's Pins Have No Points" ', was a 'side-story' that, like the earlier stories set at Mrs Dalloway's party, grew directly out of the book she had just finished. In it a young girl named Fanny Wilmot, while searching on the floor for a pin her piano teacher Julia Craye has just dropped, tells herself what she imagines to be Miss Craye's life-story. The narrative enacts the process Fanny engages in as (like Lily Briscoe telling herself the stories of the Rayleys and the Ramsays) she draws upon remembered and imagined scenes to construct the character of Julia Craye. In the end, Fanny's reflections give way to immediate impressions as she looks up and discovers Julia Craye in 'a moment of ecstasy' [*CSF* 220].

While Fanny is able to revise her story when she perceives that Julia Craye is not the lonely woman she had imagined her to be, but an intensely happy one, three stories Woolf wrote in the spring of 1929 suggest a more sceptical view of the story-teller's ability to discover the truth. In both 'The Lady in the Looking-Glass: A Reflection' and 'Three Pictures', the fiction so carefully and confidently built up by the narrator is seen at the end of the narrative to be false. The narrator of the third sketch written at this time, 'The Fascination of the Pool', must recognize another sort of limitation, as she becomes aware of something in the scene she observes which she cannot turn into narrative. All three of these short fictions anticipate Bernard's recognition in *The Waves* that 'life is not susceptible perhaps to the treatment we give it when we try to tell it' [IX], a recognition which, as we shall see, contributes to Woolf's searching exploration in that book of the functions and implications of story-telling.

Like these three stories, which are probably among those Woolf wrote to 'amuse' herself before she began the first draft of *The Waves* [*D* III 229], *Orlando*, the fantasy-biography of Vita Sackville-West, was an 'escapade' that gave Woolf a period of welcome respite after 'these serious poetic experimental books whose form is always so closely considered' [*D* III 131]. In it she satirized her own lyric vein [*D* III 131], created a hero who becomes a heroine midway through the book, and freed that androgynous seemingly immortal figure from the ravages of time which so powerfully haunt the characters in her previous fiction. 'Orlando taught me how to write a direct sentence', she reflected in November 1928, 'taught me continuity & narrative, & how to keep the realities at bay. But I purposely avoided of course any other difficulty. I never got down to my depths & made shapes square up, as I did in The Lighthouse' [*D* III 203].

Although Woolf kept the realities at bay in *Orlando*, she did in writing it begin her progress away from the psychological novel, the novel in which the novelist was, she wrote in 'The Narrow Bridge of Art' (1927), 'too prone to limit psychology to the psychology of personal intercourse' [*CE* II 225]. Orlando's relationships with the women and men in his/her life are treated as lightly and playfully as is the relationship among her multiple selves. Woolf's interest was now shifting away from the depiction in the novel of 'personal relations' to, as she wrote in 'The Narrow Bridge of Art', 'the relation of the mind to general ideas and its soliloquy in solitude. For under the dominion of the novel', she added, developing one of the central ideas in 'Impassioned Prose' (1926), we have scrutinized one part of the mind closely and left another unexplored. We have come to forget that a large and important part of life consists in our emotions toward such things as roses and nightingales, the dawn, the sunset, life, death, and fate. . . . We long for some more impersonal relationship. We long for ideas, for dreams, for imaginations, for poetry' [*CE* II 225].

She expresses a similar wish for a change of perspective in 'Women and Fiction' (1929), where she suggests that women writers may be especially well suited to achieve it, and again at the end of 'Phrases of Fiction' (1929) where, characteristically, she casts her speculations in the form of questions. The novel 'can amass details', she writes. 'But can it also select? Can it symbolize? Can it give us an epitome as well as an inventory?' she wonders [*CE* II 102]. These questions echo those Woolf had asked herself in a diary entry that contains some of her earliest thoughts about the book that would become *The Waves*:

> Why admit any thing to literature that is not poetry, by which I mean saturated? Is that not my grudge against novel[ist]s? – that they select nothing? The poets succeeding by simplifying: practically everything is left out. I want to put practically everything in; yet to saturate. [*D* III 209–10]

This new hybrid, which would combine the inclusiveness of the novel with the refinements of poetry, had no single literary antecedent. While she planned and wrote *The Waves*, she called it a 'mystical poetical work', a 'playpoem', an 'autobiography' [D III 131, 203, 229]. It would be a book poised on questions: it would have characters, but would challenge their status as characters; it would tell stories, but question the 'susceptibility' of life to such tellings; and it would counterpoint (as in 'Time Passes') the relentless chronological progress of life toward death to the cyclical rhythm of the natural world. The heuristic method of her earlier fictional works reaches new levels of complexity in *The Waves*: the questions she and her characters habitually ask about life are asked most searchingly and inclusively here.

The Waves

Woolf's desire to explore 'the relation of the mind to general ideas and its soliloquy in solitude' within the context of a work of prose fiction led her to a radical reconception both of narrative voice and of character. 'Yesterday morning I made another start on The Moths, but that won't be its title', she wrote on 25 September 1929, '& several problems cry out at once to be solved. Who thinks it? And am I outside the thinker? One wants some device which is not a trick' [D III 257]. J.W. Graham has pointed out the surprising fact that it took her three and a half years to discover the point of view she would finally use in *The Waves*.[1] The omniscient narrator of the first draft becomes in the second the narrator only of the 10 italicized passages, which Woolf called the 'interludes' [D III 285], and (one assumes) of the 12 words which recur in the nine episodes and which never vary in their formula: 'said Bernard', 'said Susan', 'said Rhoda', 'said Neville', 'said Jinny', 'said Louis'. The six voices identified by these names narrate their own perceptions, thoughts, emotions, and memories in what Woolf called a 'series of dramatic soliloquies' [D III 312]. Occasionally they seem to hear one another and even to engage in a kind of dialogue, but for the most part and until the final section, they 'speak' only to themselves.

The interludes were, Woolf felt, 'essential; so as to bridge & also give a background – the sea; insensitive nature' [D III 285]. They bridge by

1 J.W. Graham, 'Point of View in *The Waves*: Some Services of the Style', *University of Toronto Quarterly* XXXIX, 3 (April 1970), p. 200. Reprinted in Thomas S.W. Lewis, ed., *Virginia Woolf: A Collection of Criticism* (New York: McGraw-Hill, 1975). See also Graham's Introduction to *The Waves: The Two Holograph Drafts*.

chronicling the progress of a day from pre-dawn at the beginning of the first interlude, to mid-day in the fifth, to total darkness at the end of the ninth. Only the tenth italicized passage, the single sentence with which the book ends, is neither situated in time nor narrated in the present tense. Like an intricate musical theme, the interludes recur with variations at regular intervals to counterpoint the development of the main melody, the progress through time of the lives of the six speakers.

The interludes provide a setting from which the six speakers seem to emerge in the first episode and to which Bernard returns in memory in the ninth. No narrator intrudes into their soliloquies to place them in the house and garden described in the italicized passages or, as they grow older, to tell the reader the facts of their lives. (In a note for one of the episodes Woolf wrote, 'the rhythmic design should dominate the facts'.[2]) What we know of these we must assemble from what they say. Their few references to specific places tell us, for example, that Bernard, Neville, and Louis go to Cambridge,[3] that Susan marries and lives somewhere in the country, that as an adult Jinny immerses herself in the glittering social life of London where Rhoda, and, after university, the three male speakers also live. Their farewell dinner for Percival is held in a French restaurant in London (at the same restaurant, it may be, where Bernard has dinner in the final episode) and their reunion dinner at Hampton Court; Percival dies somewhere in India.

It is significant that in a book which the author meant to be read 'not as a novel' and in which the details of setting are relatively few, there is nevertheless so much residual realism. The speakers are differentiated not only by name, but also by distinctive habits of mind, some of which are expressed in terms that become *leitmotifs* as they recur with slight variations (as in Wagnerian opera) and contribute both to the presentation of each speaker and to the rhythm of the work as a whole. These recurring *leitmotifs* (Rhoda's 'I have no face'; Louis's 'my father a banker in Brisbane'; Bernard's comforting assumption that 'Tuesday follows Monday', for example) reflect Woolf's growing interest in caricature. 'What I now think (about the Waves)', she wrote in April 1930, as she was completing the first draft, 'is that I can give in a very few strokes the essentials of a person's character. It should be done boldly,

2 *The Two Holograph Drafts*, p. 755.
3 Avrom Fleishman, in *Virginia Woolf: A Critical Reading* (Baltimore: Johns Hopkins University Press, 1975), notes that the reference to Byron's tree [III] identifies the university as Cambridge (p. 151).

almost as caricature' [*D* III 300]. This extension of her earlier use of character types is central to her movement away from the psychological novel with its focus on personal relationships and on the complexity of the individual personality.[4] The self-narration these six speakers relentlessly engage in continually expands from private preoccupations (often marked by *leitmotifs*) to general ones, from the personal to the impersonal, from questions about their own lives to larger questions about being alive and thus about being and about life itself. Hence Woolf could think of *The Waves* as 'autobiography' while insisting that the childhood of the first section 'must not be *my* childhood' [*D* III 236]. This would be the life of anyone, and of no one.

Working in counterpoint to the details that distinguish the six speakers from one another are the many images and perceptions they share. As we have seen, Woolf uses shared images and perceptions to relate characters on a psychological or spiritual level in *Mrs Dalloway* and *To the Lighthouse*; now she extends that technique by making her speakers share as well a common and unchanging discourse: all six speak the same 'purebred prose' from childhood to middle age [*L* IV 381]. When Woolf wondered if *The Waves* could be read consecutively, she may have been thinking in part about the difficulty readers have, despite the bold strokes of caricature, distinguishing one speaker from another. The speakers contribute to this blurring of differences by experiencing it themselves; they know themselves as separate people and yet acknowledge at times the dissolution of the barriers between them. During the farewell dinner, for example, Percival, who has no voice in the text, is perceived as the 'background' against which the others compose themselves into one whole. ' "It is Percival," said Louis, "sitting silent, . . . who makes us aware that these attempts to say, 'I am this, I am that,' which we make, coming together, like separated parts of one body and soul, are false. . . . From the desire to be separate we have laid stress upon our faults, and what is particular to us. But there is a chain whirling round, round, in a steel-blue circle beneath" ' [IV]. As Bernard attempts in the final episode to describe 'this globe, full of figures' which is his life, he echoes Louis's sense of their unity: ' "And now I ask, 'Who am I?' I have been talking of Bernard, Neville, Jinny, Susan, Rhoda and Louis. Am I all of them? Am I one and distinct? I do not know. We sat here together. But now Percival is dead, and Rhoda is dead; we are divided; we are not here. Yet

---

4 See J.W. Graham, 'The "Caricature Value" of Parody and Fantasy in *Orlando* in *Virginia Woolf*': *A Collection of Critical Essays*, ed. Claire Sprague (Englewood Cliffs, NJ: Prentice-Hall, 1971), pp. 101–16.

I cannot find any obstacle separating us. There is no division between me and them." '5

In a work in which the functions of narrator and character are so radically reconceived, what happens to the event and to the story, the sequence of events which the writer shapes into a plot? 'I am not trying to tell a story', Woolf noted before she began the first draft. 'I can tell stories', she added. 'But thats not it' [*D* III 229–30]. By the time she had begun the second draft, her alternative to telling a story was clear to her. 'I am writing [*The Waves*] to a rhythm and not to a plot', she told Ethel Smyth in August 1930. 'And thus though the rhythmical is more natural to me than the narrative, it is completely opposed to the tradition of fiction and I am casting about all the time for some rope to throw to the reader' [*L* IV 204]. 'Writing to a rhythm' means, for one thing, linking the natural rhythms enacted in the interludes – the rise and fall of the waves, the diurnal and seasonal cycles – to the lives of the six speakers as they pass from childhood to middle age. Further, the book's nine episodes are related to one another in a rhythmical design, one that imitates the movement of the waves and also recalls the movement from slow to fast to slow time in the three parts of *To the Lighthouse*. The first three episodes moved forward in time; the fourth stops as they all gather for the farewell dinner for Percival; the next three episodes again move forward as the speakers grow older; in the eighth the narrative again pauses as they assemble for the second reunion dinner; and in the ninth episode, Bernard gives a long after-dinner speech, a summing up which, wave-like, both moves backward as he remembers their pasts and forward as, at the end, he confronts the future.

The rhythm Woolf was writing to is enacted not only in the design of the book as a whole, but it is also present in the style – in the dense image patterns and in the rhythmical cadences of the prose – and in the changing states of mind of the speakers, which that style records. That Woolf thought of these states of mind in terms of rhythm is clear from some notes she made for episode seven. 'That there are waves, or reasons in life, by wh. life is marked', she wrote in her notebook, 'a rounding off, wh. has nothing to do with birth, & events. A natural finishing . . . One observes these rhythms in oneself'.6 Like Woolf, the speakers observe these internal rhythms and their narration of them as

5 Virginia Woolf told G.L. Dickinson, 'But I did mean that in some vague way we are the same person, and not separate people. The six characters were supposed to be one' [*L* IV 397].
6 *The Two Holograph Drafts*, p. 758.

they occur and as they are remembered further contributes to the rhythmical design of the whole. Like the facts of their lives, which are seldom narrated, events occur offstage, as in 'Time Passes', and only when they affect the rhythms of being are they mentioned by the speakers.

One example of this treatment of events is the presentation of Percival's death, the central event in the book. Percival has no voice in the text and thus is known to us only through the reflections of the others. In their lives, and in the narrative, he functions as both a person and a symbol. As a person he is a caricature of the school hero, the handsome, athletic, unreflective boy and then young man whom others imitate, admire, and love. In some ways he is another Jacob Flanders, but without, it seems, Jacob's intelligence. ' "He takes my devotion", Neville says, ' "he accepts my tremulous, no doubt abject offering, mixed with contempt as it is for his mind" ' [II]. Although no one makes direct reference to his namesake, the legendary grail knight, Bernard does cast Percival in the role of hero: he is the medieval commander who will die in battle [II], the 'captain' to this group of six 'soldiers' [IV], a 'God' Bernard says, surely with some irony, who will help to bring justice and order to India [IV]. As the heroic man of action, he is the centre of this highly self-conscious circle of friends, the presence who, as Louis says, makes them realize that they are one. Thus his sudden death is devastating, for not only does it remove a friend and unifying presence from their lives, but, like the deaths in Woolf's earlier narratives, it forces them to contemplate the reality of death itself.

We learn of his death at the centre of the book, the opening of the fifth episode. ' "He is dead," said Neville. "He fell. His horse tripped. He was thrown" '. Neville announces Percival's death by stating the facts he had learned from a telegram. His thoughts quickly extend beyond these however, as he enters imaginatively into the scene, much as Clarissa Dalloway does when she learns of Septimus Warren Smith's death. ' "His horse stumbled; he was thrown. The flashing trees and white rails went up in a shower. There was a surge; a drumming in his ears. Then the blow; the world crashed; he breathed heavily. He died where he fell" ' [V]. The focus then shifts from the story of Percival's death to the profound effects it has on the others. This single death quickly becomes symbolic of all deaths – ' "Percival has died (he died in Egypt; he died in Greece; all deaths are one death" '), Louis says [VI] – and of unconsolable loss. Bernard's moving line, ' "No lullabye has ever occurred to me capable of singing him to rest" ' [IX], contributes to the exploration in the book of those parts of life that lie outside the boundaries of stories and the comforts of language.

Woolf extends the critique of story implicit in her experimental narrative methods through Bernard's explicit comments on his self-assumed role as story-teller. As a child, Bernard is confident that, as Neville says, he can ' "describe what we have all seen so that it becomes a sequence. Bernard says there is always a story" ' [II]. Yet Bernard's confidence is challenged even at this early stage by moments when he fails to find a sequence. Neville records one of these: ' "The sentence tails off feebly. Yes, the appalling moment has come when Bernard's power fails him and there is no longer any sequence and he sags and twiddles a bit of string and falls silent, . . . Among the tortures and devastations of life is this then – our friends are not able to finish their stories" ' [II]. Although significant, this moment does not undermine Bernard's belief that he will be ' "called upon to provide, some winter's night, a meaning for all my observations – a line that runs from one to another, a summing up that completes" ' [IV].

By the time this occasion finally arrives, Bernard has come sometimes ' "to doubt if there are stories" ' [IV], to question whether ' "the true story, the one story to which all these phrases refer" ' can be told [VII], or whether, if told, it can be distinguished among the innumerable stories he tells: ' "Waves of hands, hesitations at street corners, someone dropping a cigarette into the gutter – all are stories. But which is the true story? That I do not know" ' [VIII]. Thus when at the opening of episode nine he begins to explain to his silent dinner companion ' "the meaning of my life" ' he knows that he cannot do so. ' "But in order to make you understand, to give you my life, I must tell you a story – and there are so many, and so many – stories of childhood, stories of school, love, marriage, death and so on; and none of them are true." '

Behind this assertion and acting as the pivot of Bernard's summing up, is his memory of the day when ' "the rhythm stopped" ' and he became for a short time ' "a man without a self" '. The self that disappeared is the self that had lived within the comforting rhythms of daily life (' "Tuesday follows Monday" ') and had been confidently commemorating the orderly sequences of that life in stories. ' "How can I proceed now" ', he had asked himself, ' "without a self, weightless and visionless, . . . without illusion?" ' The world Bernard saw 'without a self' is the vision that Lily Briscoe and now Rhoda seek – ' "the thing that lies beneath the semblance of the thing" ' [V] – the reality that lies, as Woolf says in 'On Not Knowing Greek', 'on the far side of language'

[CE I 7]. ' "But how describe the world seen without a self?" ' Bernard asks. ' "There are no words. Blue, red – even they distract, even they hide with thickness instead of letting the light through." ' Bernard can only describe what he saw once his self has returned ' "with all its train of phantom phrases" ' and that vision has become a memory.

> 'But for a moment I had sat on the turf somewhere high above the flow of the sea and the sound of the woods, had seen the house, the garden and the waves breaking. The old nurse who turns the pages of the picture-book had stopped and had said, "Look. This is the truth." '

Bernard evokes the world of the interludes,but in striking contrast to the richly metaphoric language of those passages, his prose is simple and unadorned. Like the old nurse who shows him a 'picture-book', Bernard presents the natural world seen as it exists independent of him. This is perhaps as close as words can bring him to reality.

Thus Bernard knows that his stories are not true because he has experienced a truth that stories, and the language used to tell them, cannot fully express. He must tell his stories, for he continues to live within the sequences of time and to narrate his life to himself as he lives it, but his awareness of a state of being in which 'I' is 'forgotten' works as a continuous undertow, a counter impulse leading him away from stories and beautiful phrases to 'words of one syllable', to a 'howl; a cry', and finally, if briefly, to silence. ' "How much better is silence" ', he says near the end of his monologue, ' "the coffee-cup, the table. . . . things in themselves, myself being myself." '

The contradictory impulses that shape the rhythm of Bernard's monologue can be linked to the questions Woolf asked herself in a diary entry which is central to the inquiry undertaken in *The Waves.* This was written on 4 January 1929, a few months before she began the first draft of *The Waves.*

> Now is life very solid, or very shifting? I am haunted by the two contradictions. This has gone on for ever: will last for ever; goes down to the bottom of the world – this moment I stand on. Also it is transitory, flying, diaphanous. I shall pass like a cloud on the waves. Perhaps it may be that though we change; one flying after another, so quick, so quick, yet we are somehow successive, & continuous – we human beings; & show the light through. But what is the light? [D III 218]

Woolf's provisional answer to her first question seems to be that life is both solid and shifting, that although 'we change', we are at the same time part of an unchanging reality sometimes glimpsed in 'moments of vision', moments when we 'show the light through'. Bernard experienced such a transparency when he 'walked unshadowed', as does Rhoda, whose repeated statement, ' "I have no face" ', indicates how tenuous her sense of self is. ' "Yet there are moments when the walls of the mind grow thin" ', she says in one of the central passages in the book,

> 'when nothing is unabsorbed, and I could fancy that we might blow so vast a bubble that the sun might set and rise in it and we might take the blue of midday and the black of midnight and be cast off and escape from here and now.' [VIII]

The escape from here and now is also an escape from the self, an expansion into a radical anonymity which Rhoda welcomes and finally sustains in death. Bernard, who has called Rhoda his opposite, knows after his brief loss of self the attraction, but also the terror, of that loss. After having recalled that experience, he echoes Woolf's second question, 'But what is the light?', in a question he too leaves unanswered: ' "What does the central shadow hold? Something? Nothing? I do not know." ' The light and the shadow are two aspects of the same thing, the 'essence of reality' Woolf was attempting to reach in *The Waves*, a book which was written, she later said, 'with no wish except to make something solid' [*L* VI 360].

Immediately after she had written the last words of the second draft of *The Waves*, on 7 February 1931, Woolf recorded in her diary that the book was 'not merely finished, but rounded off, completed, the thing stated' [*D* IV 10]. The distinction she implies here between two kinds of conclusions can be linked to the treatment of story-telling in *The Waves*. The story is not abandoned, but absorbed into a larger, more inclusive text, one in which endings and beginnings do not enclose a sequential narrative of events, but mark points of emphasis in a rhythmical design. Bernard recognizes this expansion of context when he emerges from the restaurant and celebrates the ' "general awakening" ' of another day: ' "Yes, this is the eternal renewal, the incessant rise and fall and fall and rise again." ' His figure is similarly absorbed into a larger context now as he is transformed from a middle-aged man standing in ' "the usual street" ' into a mythic hero, Percival reborn, who proclaims he ' "will fling" ' himself ' "unvanquished and unyielding" ' against Death, and who then disappears from the narrative.

The final line of the book – '*The waves broke on the shore*' – shifts the perspective once more as the natural world and its rhythms, with which the book began and which was evoked in Bernard's vision of the 'truth', is again brought into the foreground. Woolf achieves in these final passages the sort of expansion E.M. Forster describes at the close of his chapter on rhythm in *Aspects of the Novel*: 'When the symphony is over we feel that the notes and tunes composing it have been liberated, they have found in the rhythm of the whole their individual freedom. Cannot the novel be like that?'[7] Woolf would probably have answered, Yes, it can. 'What interests me in the last stage', she wrote in her diary on 7 February 1931, 'was the freedom & boldness with which my imagination picked up used & tossed aside all the images & symbols which I had prepared. I am sure that this is the right way of using them – not in set pieces, as I had tried at first, coherently, but simply as images; never making them work out; only suggest. Thus I hope to have kept the sound of the sea & the birds, dawn, & garden subconsciously present, doing their work under ground' [*D* IV 10–11]. Like themes in music, Woolf's images and symbols recur and are subtly altered by their changing contexts. Their repetition and variation contribute to the 'rhythm of the whole', the expanding and contracting impulses of what Louis calls ' "the central rhythm, . . . the common mainspring" ' [III] which shapes *The Waves*. The contraction of the book's brief final line checks, but does not silence, the expansive impulse embodied in Bernard's lyrical and heroic defiance of Death.

6

A Re-created World: *The Years* and *Between the Acts*

The Years

'No critic ever gives full weight to the desire of the mind for change', Woolf noted in her diary in January 1933 [*D* IV 145]. That desire is apparent when we turn from *The Waves* to *The Years*. One of the major problems that faced her in writing this book, in which, she said, her characters would be turned 'towards society, not private life' [*L* VI 116], was how to 'give ordinary waking Arnold Bennett life the form of art?' [*D* IV 161]. She again foresaw her book as a hybrid, one that would give 'facts, as well as the vision', as she put it, 'The Waves going on simultaneously with Night & Day' [*D* IV 151–2]. She thought at first that she could alternate fictional scenes depicting the life of the Pargiter family with 'interchapters', essays in which she would discuss the society in which they live, but she soon found this method uncongenial and abandoned it. There were 'to be millions of ideas but no preaching' [*D* IV 152] in this book. As she continued to work on it, she found it tending 'more & more . . . to drama' [*D* IV 168]. This was not a 'playpoem', however. She was delighting in the 'gold' to be found 'in externality' [*D* IV 133] and she drew on the methods dramatists use to maintain 'contact with the surface' [*D* IV 207]: the interplay of dialogue, gestures, and actions through which characters present themselves and their stories to each other and to the audience.

Woolf's return to the methods of traditional realism is reflected in the structure of *The Years*. The narrative is divided into 11 sections, each dated and each introduced by a few paragraphs in which the month or season of the year is described. As the following list shows, the years seem to have been chosen almost at random and, in sharp contrast to *The Waves*, the introductory descriptive passages form no overarching pattern: 1880 (spring), 1891 (autumn), 1907 (summer), 1908 (March), 1910 (spring), 1911 (August), 1913 (January), 1914 (spring), 1917 (winter), 1918 (November), Present Day (summer). These facts are important to her portrayal of the Pargiters' lives, but they do not in themselves suggest any external design, any plot, giving meaning to those lives.

Yet *The Years* is not a conventional realistic novel. As in her previous works, Woolf explores here some of the implications and limitations of the narrative methods she is using. For example, the absent years in this chronicle are the most obvious of many absences in the book. The 'chasms in the continuity of our ways' which the narrator of *Jacob's Room* describes and which seem enacted in the continual shifts of perspective and embodied in the many spaces that divide the separate scenes in that book, constantly interrupt the progress of the narrative in *The Years*. Not only do spaces on the page again divide one scene from another, but within those scenes moments of silence continually break into the narrative. These are especially noticeable when they concern story-telling. ' "Tell us that story, Mama" ', Sara urges her mother. ' "Not tonight" ', her mother replies. '. . . "I will tell you the true story another time," she said freeing herself from her daughter's grasp. . . . "She won't tell us," said Maggie, picking up her gloves' [1907]. Maggie is right. Eugenie's 'true story' remains untold. Requests for stories recur and are denied with frustrating frequency. 'And then?' one character will prompt another, in an attempt to complete a story. In some scenes stories are told but not narrated, thus leaving the reader (as it were) out of earshot. In others, characters try to speak, but are interrupted and thus are unable, like Bernard, to finish their stories.[1]

The fragmentation and discontinuity created in the narrative by the untold, unheard, and unfinished stories, by the spaces on the page, and by the omitted years in the Pargiter family chronicle are counterpointed, as in Woolf's previous fiction, by a design formed by the repetition of images, phrases, gestures, incidents and ideas. This internal design is closely linked to the notion, also explored in *The Voyage Out* and *Night and Day*, that there may be a pattern underlying

1 I am indebted to Rachel Blau DuPlessis's discussion of this aspect of *The Years* in *Writing Beyond the Ending: Narrative Strategies of Twentieth-Century Women Writers* (Bloomington: University of Indiana Press, 1985), pp. 162–77.

the apparently episodic randomness of human life. Eleanor is particularly concerned with this possibility, which she associates with a drawing she habitually makes of a dot with spokes radiating from it. When she is younger, this image expresses the dull, predictable routine of her life [1910], but later, the image has more positive and far-reaching implications. 'But how did they compose what people called a life?' she wonders. 'Perhaps there's "I" at the middle of it, she thought; a knot; a centre; and again she saw herself sitting at her table drawing on the blotting-paper, digging little holes from which spokes radiated.' A moment later she extends this idea by thinking again about repetition. This time, however, instead of feeling entrapped by the monotony of the things people repeatedly do and say, she finds this repetition liberating. 'Does everything then come over again a little differently? she thought. If so, is there a pattern; a theme, recurring, like music; half remembered, half forseen? . . . But who makes it? Who thinks it? Her mind slipped. She could not finish her thought' [Present Day].

Eleanor's drawing recalls Clarissa Dalloway's diamond-imaged, multi-faceted self, with the dot at the centre in this instance representing the self and the spokes radiating from it all the traces, as Woolf called them in 'A Sketch of the Past', that experience scores in our memories.[2] In *The Years*, as in *The Voyage Out* and *Night and Day*, Woolf explores the ways that the inevitable recurrence of similar events in an individual's life may testify to the presence in it of some informing pattern. Early in the narrative, for example, Delia and Milly watch from the window as a cab stops two doors down the street. A young man gets out, pays the driver, and enters the house. ' "Don't be caught looking," ' Eleanor warns them [1880]. At the end of the book this scene is repeated, only this time it is Eleanor who watches and instead of a young man alone, a man and a woman emerge from the cab and enter the house, not as visitors, it seems, but as occupants. ' "There," Eleanor murmured, . . . "There!" she repeated, . . . Then she turned round into the room. "And now?" she said, . . . "And now?" ' The book then closes with a single sentence: 'The sun had risen, and the sky above the houses wore an air of extraordinary beauty, simplicity and peace.'

As we have seen, Woolf's description in *A Room of One's Own* of a scene viewed from a window served as an example of the mind's ability to project its own rhythms on to the external world. In *The Years*, the scene seems intended to suggest continuity, a rhythm of recurrence

2 'A Sketch of the Past', p. 67.

which does not depend upon the perceptions of the observer and which gives shape to the individual life. Eleanor clearly finds the moment deeply satisfying. Her exclamation recalls the triumphant endings of Mrs Dalloway and To the Lighthouse and suggests that something has been achieved. Her final question, echoing as it does the recurring 'And then?' of the other characters, followed by the description of the dawn with which the book ends, sounds a note more emphatically anticipatory and optimistic than we have heard at the close of any of Woolf's novels since Night and Day. Yet while this scene may confirm for Eleanor, and for the reader, the existence of a pattern in the individual life, the question 'who makes it', and thus what it ultimately means, remains unanswered, another unfinished story. The narrator, characteristically, offers no comment, but in distancing us from the characters with the final sentence, she may be suggesting, as Woolf has in her previous fiction, that beyond the rhythms discoverable in the individual life, the only pattern giving shape to life itself is that created by the rhythms of the natural world. The dot with spokes radiating from it may be an image not only of the self at the centre of its world, but also, when viewed from a perspective that transcends the self, an image of the sun, whose cycles mark persistently and indifferently, the complex process of our life in time.

Eleanor's unfinished thoughts, like the many unfinished stories in the narrative, contribute to the heuristic method and the resistance to closure that inform Woolf's treatment of character in The Years. Eleanor's notion that 'I' may be at the centre is complicated by the recurring inquiry other characters make into the nature of 'I' itself. ' "What's 'I'?" ' Sara asks repeatedly [1907]; 'But what is this moment; and what are we?' wonders Peggy [Present Day], whose more inclusive vision anticipates Woolf's intentions for Between the Acts: ' "I" rejected: "We" substituted' [D V 135]. Woolf puts 'I' at the centre of the narrative in that the foreground is dominated by the speech, thoughts, and actions of the characters; but in another sense, she has displaced the 'I', for no one character resides at the centre of this text and the questions characters pose about the nature of the 'I' are not linked, as they are in Woolf's earlier works, to an extended inquiry into the many facets of the individual self. The cast of characters in The Years is large; some who may seem central at one point, such as Abel Pargiter or Kitty Malone, fade into the background in later scenes or disappear altogether. Eleanor comes closest to being the central character, but she has neither the insistent presence of Mrs Dalloway and Mrs Ramsay, nor the elusive importance to others of Jacob or Percival. A similar displacement of the central 'I' will occur again in Woolf's last novel.

Between the Acts

The Years was published in March 1937, and *Three Guineas*, Woolf's powerful sequel to *A Room of One's Own*, in June 1938. In April of that year, she had begun to write the biography of Roger Fry, which she would publish in July 1940. During this period she was also writing short stories, some for publication in *Harper's Bazaar* and others which she would leave unpublished, along with essays and reviews. Among the latter was 'The Leaning Tower' (1940), an important essay in which she assessed, from her perspective as a woman without a university degree and thus, as she says in *Three Guineas* an 'outsider', and with some help from her recent reading of Freud, the effects of class and education on contemporary male writers. She also began to write a memoir, 'A Sketch of the Past', which, like two extended essays also begun at this time, 'Anon' and 'The Reader', she would leave unfinished at her death.[3] And soon after she began to write *Roger Fry*, she also began work on *Pointz Hall*, the book that would become *Between the Acts*.

Woolf found writing the biography of Fry a 'drudgery' and turned to *Pointz Hall* as a source of relaxation, much as years before she had given her imagination free play in 'The Mark on the Wall' while straining under the discipline of writing *Night and Day*. Woolf's diary also makes it clear that *Pointz Hall* provided a diversion from the war, the events and effects of which dominate the moving entries of this period. The war had taken away 'the outer wall of security', she wrote in June 1940. 'No echo comes back. I have no surroundings.' '. . . the writing "I", has vanished', she had noted two weeks earlier. 'No audience. No echo. Thats part of one's death' [D v 299, 293]. In *Between the Acts* she creates an audience to replace the actual one she felt she had lost. And in the dramatist, Miss La Trobe, who curses all audiences as 'the devil', she presents a comic and profound portrait of the 'writing "I" ' at work.

Woolf called *Between the Acts* a 'medley' [D v 193]. In it a fictional narrative, which like *Mrs Dalloway* covers the limited time-span of 24 hours, frames the performance of a village pageant, which like *Orlando* spans several centuries. Talk of painting and of poetry, along

3 ' "Anon" and "The Reader": Virginia Woolf's Last Essays', ed. Brenda R. Silver, *Twentieth Century Literature* 25.3/4 (Fall/Winter 1979), pp. 356–441.

with fragments of verse and song, occur in the framing-narrative, while the pageant includes not only poetry, prose, and pantomime, but music and dance, too. *Between the Acts* is also a 'medley' in a more general sense, for many of the barriers that divide person from person – barriers of reticence, decorum, class, and sex, for example – are challenged and often broken down as the book proceeds. Nature, viewed as indifferent to human concerns in Woolf's earlier works, here plays a major part in them. Woolf's 'growing detachment from the hierarchy, the patriarchy' [D V 347], expressed so forcefully in *Three Guineas*, is reflected in the disruption of these barriers and also lies behind this amusing, deeply serious book.

As in *The Years*, Woolf draws on and draws our attention to the methods of both the dramatist and the novelist to present her characters. While the players in the pageant attempt to play the parts Miss La Trobe has cast them in, their friends in the audience delight in pointing out to one another the true identity of their costumed neighbours, thus giving them in a sense two roles to play. Such alternating fusion and separation of the actor and his or her part also occurs in the framing-narrative which develops before, between, and after the pageant's four acts. Here Woolf uses not only gesture and speech, but also narrated and quoted monologue, along with the narrator's own comments, to present her characters. Like Miss La Trobe's characters, the major actors in the framing-narrative have been drawn in part with the bold strokes of caricature, for the attitudes they strike are often familiar ones, especially within Woolf's fictional world. In addition, their preoccupations are closely tied to the larger concerns of the book.

The family patriarch, Bart Oliver, dreams of his former life in India and the glories of the lost Empire, a period that comes in for particularly satirical treatment in the pageant's Victorian scene. His sister Lucy Swithin, whose faith in Christianity he chides, cannot 'fix her gaze' very clearly or long on the present moment; like Mrs Ramsay, she engages in 'one-making', while Bart, like Mr Ramsay with his sequential view of knowledge, takes pride in being what he calls a 'separatist'. Mrs Swithin's response to the pageant illustrates the contrast between brother and sister. ' "The Victorians," Mrs Swithin mused. "I don't believe," she said with her odd little smile, "that there ever were such people. Only you and me and William dressed differently." "You don't believe in history," said William' [203]. Bart's daughter-in-law, Isa, believes intensely in history and much of her emotional life seems engaged in the effort to escape it. ' "That was the burden," she mused, "laid on me in the cradle; murmured by waves; breathed by restless elm trees; crooned by singing women; what we must remember; what we would forget" ' [182]. In contrast to Isa, Mrs Manressa, the self-proclaimed, self-delighting 'wild child of nature', enjoys an expansive freedom from these burdens, while Miss La Trobe, artist, lesbian, and outsider in this small community, transforms the past (with parodic intent) into art. For Isa's virile stockbroker husband Giles ('the father of my children' she reminds herself, casting him in one of his roles), the burden of the past is manifested in the coming war and, on the smaller domestic stage, in the unexplained tensions in his marriage. He focuses some of his irritation on Mrs Manressa's friend William Dodge, a homosexual burdened with the failures of his own past. The characters' awareness of the familiar roles they play and their tendency to cast those around them in supporting parts, like the success with which Miss La Trobe implicates the audience in her unfolding pageant, contributes to the book's pervasive theatricality.

The narrator plays the most complex role of all in this rich medley of interwoven stories. At times she recalls the intrusive narrator of *Jacob's Room* as she indulges in 'character-mongering' to sketch in the characters' pasts and personalities and to offer lively commentaries on their actions. At other times she effaces herself as she moves into the characters' minds, as in *Mrs Dalloway*, *To the Lighthouse*, and *The Years*, to quote or narrate their thoughts and perceptions. At some points the narrator seems to abandon her omniscience and to speak simply as another member of the audience; at others she disappears altogether and the audience, a medley of anonymous voices, takes over the narration, commenting chorus-like on the play and the events and ideas it calls up. Finally, while retaining a distinct voice, the narrator periodically distances herself from the pageant and the characters to concern herself not with telling stories, but with conveying what Woolf might have called a perception of reality. Her description of the empty dining room, to which I shall return in a moment, is a central example of this.

Although Woolf has again (as in *Mrs Dalloway*) eliminated the chapter as a narrative unit, the shifts in the narrator's tone and perspective and the alternation between framing-narrative and pageant, continually break the sequence of the narrative. ' "Curse! Blast! Damn 'em!" ' Miss La Trobe rages when the first interval interrupts the pageant. 'Just as she had brewed emotion, she spilt it' [113]. Such breaks draw attention to the most obvious meaning of the title, for it is during these intervals that the stories of the characters in the framing-narrative resume centre stage. These stories are, in turn, interrupted by the pageant; thus with a shift of perspective, the acts of the pageant become the intervals and the intervals become the play. From a contemporary perspective, the title can refer to this June day in 1939, an interval of fragile peace between two acts of war; from a more inclusive historical perspective, it is suggestive of the long period between the beginning of time, the creation, and its anticipated end, the apocalypse. And from the perspective of the narration, which I would like to turn to next, the title can suggest the silence, sometimes expressive and sometimes merely empty, which, as Bernard so memorably discovered, frames all speech and all stories.

Early in the book the narrator describes two pictures which hang in the dining room at Pointz Hall.

> Two pictures hung opposite the window. In real life they had never met, the long lady and the man holding his horse by the rein. The lady was a picture, bought by Oliver because he liked the picture; the man was an ancestor. He had a name.

The narrator then imagines the ancestor giving instructions to the painter and concludes:

> He was a talk producer, that ancestor. But the lady was a picture. In her yellow robe, leaning, with a pillar to support her, a silver arrow in her hand, and a feather in her hair, she led the eye up, down, from the curve to the straight, through glades of greenery and shades of silver, dun and rose into silence. The room was empty.

'Yet it may be', one of the speakers in Woolf's essay 'Walter Sickert' (1934) says, 'that there is a zone of silence in the middle of every art' [*CE* II 236]. The silence at the centre of this picture complements the silence of the empty room in which it hangs.

> Empty, empty, empty; silent, silent, silent. The room was a shell, singing of what was before time was; a vase stood in the heart of the house, alabaster, smooth, cold, holding the still, distilled essence of emptiness, silence. [46–7]

In contrast to the more profound silence of the alabaster vase in the library ('the heart of the house', one of the Olivers' guests called it), the silence of the empty room, 'singing of what was before time was', is potential with all sound.

More commonplace and familiar silences occur, often with comic effect, in the conversations that take place in the framing-narrative. During lunch, for example, Isa surveys the newly arrived Mrs Manressa. ' "Or what are your rings for, and your nails, and that really adorable little straw hat?" said Isabella addressing Mrs Manressa silently and thereby making silence add its unmistakable contribution to talk' [49–50]. As in Woolf's previous narratives, these silent comments are sometimes 'heard' by others and, fortunately, sometimes not.

Both silence and emptiness continually plague Miss La Trobe. Waiting for the pageant to begin or resume, the members of the audience grow restive as they face the empty stage. Worse than these moments are those, such as one that occurs in the midst of the Restoration scene, when first the villagers' singing cannot be heard and then, as they drift away, the stage remains unaccountably empty. 'Miss La Trobe leant against the tree, paralysed. Her power had left her. Beads of perspiration broke on her forehead. Illusion had failed. "This is death," she murmured, "death" ' [165]. This would have been a solemn moment in one of Woolf's earlier books, but here Miss La Trobe's dilemma, real though it is, achieves a quick and comic resolution. The cows in an adjacent field begin to bellow 'as if Eros had planted his dart in their flanks and goaded them to fury.' Their loud 'dumb yearning' burlesques the love stories being told in both the pageant and the framing-narrative: 'The cows annihilated the gap; bridged the distance; filled the emptiness and continued the emotion. Miss La Trobe waved her hand ecstatically at the cows. "Thank Heaven!" she exclaimed' [165–6].

The human need not only to fill the silence, but to fill it with stories, amusingly illustrated here by the role as victims of Eros the cows are made fortuitously to play, seems to impose the inescapable burden of narration on the artist. This imposition becomes most clear near the end of the pageant when Miss La Trobe tries a radical experiment with minimalist drama.

> After Vic.' she had written, 'try ten mins. of present time. Swallows, cows etc.' She wanted to expose them, as it were, to douche them, with present-time reality. But something was going wrong with the experiment. 'Reality too strong,' she muttered. 'Curse 'em!' She felt everything they felt. Audiences were the devil. O to write a play without an audience – *the* play. [209–10]

The audience is again rescued from this exposure to reality by nature, for the rain that has held off all day now unexpectedly falls. And as before, the narrator and the characters read this natural event as a scene in the human drama. 'Down it poured like all the people in the world weeping', the narrator says. 'Tears. Tears. Tears' [210].

This brief flood of tears serves as an appropriate prelude to the final scene, which begins with a pantomime representing the reconstruction that followed the First World War. Mr Page, the reporter, describes it for us: 'Civilization (the wall) in ruins; rebuilt (witness man with hod) by human effort; witness also woman handing bricks. Any fool could grasp that" ' [212]. The intention of Miss La Trobe's final scene is not so easy for the audience to grasp, however. Again taking the risk of abandoning narrative, she confronts her audience with a fragmented, jostling, chaotic, and silent wall of mirrors. 'Mopping, mowing, whisking, frisking, the looking glasses darted, flashed, exposed' [214]. With the exception of Mrs Manressa, who takes the opportunity to touch up her lipstick, the people in the front rows, facing themselves in this 'wilderness of mirrors',[4] are indignant; those behind them, seeing the others so unceremoniously exposed, are, like the players, amused. The audience has become the play, and the players the audience.

In her brief epilogue, spoken from the bushes in an 'anonymous bray', Miss La Trobe challenges the audience to admit that '*All you can see of yourselves is scraps, orts and fragments?*' [220].[5] The music that follows, however, like Reverend Streatfield, who is left with the unenviable job of summing up, suggests a contrary unifying vision. ' "We act different parts" ', he observes, ' "but are the same. . . . Scraps, orts and fragments! Surely, we should unite?" ' [224–5]. The 12 airplanes that cut 'opportunity' in two, like the truncated words, 'un' and 'dis', heard as the audience leave, imply that such unification may be more difficult to achieve than he is able to see.

Miss La Trobe is, to borrow the distinction Bart makes between himself and his sister, both a separatist and a unifier. 'What is her game? To disrupt?' an anonymous voice asks [213]. In her parody of familiar stories of love and self-interest, in her attempt at the end of the pageant to escape those stories and confront the audience with reality and themselves, Miss La Trobe has sought, as Isa recognized, to cut the 'knot' in the centre, to let silence and emptiness become, perhaps, the prologue to a radical new story. Her pageant performs the disruption, the decreation, which must precede recreation. 'Ah, but she was not merely a twitcher of individual strings;' the narrator says, 'she was one who seethes wandering bodies and floating voices in a cauldron, and makes rise up from its amorphous mass a re-created world' [180].

4 T.S. Eliot, 'Gerontion'
5 Miss La Trobe has adopted lines from Troilus's bitter account of the changed Cressida: 'The fractions of her faith, orts of her love, / The fragments, scraps, the bits and greasy relics / Of her o'ereaten faith are bound to Diomed.' William Shakespeare, *Troilus and Cressida*, V, ii, 193–5.

The exchange between disruption and harmony, chaos and creation, complements that between silence and sound, emptiness and fulness; these work in subtle counterpoint to form the underlying rhythm in *Between the Acts*, one that can be seen as a variant of the systaltic rhythm that informs *Jacob's Room*, *Mrs Dalloway*, *To the Lighthouse*, and *The Waves*. By making the emphasis fall on degeneration and discord, Woolf gives the book an apocalyptic quality; like Yeats in 'The Second Coming', Lawrence in *Women in Love*, and Eliot in 'Gerontion' and *The Waste Land*, she presents a fractured world which seems on the brink of ruin. ' "What we need is a centre" ', someone in the audience observes. ' "Something to bring us all together" ' [231]. That a 're-created world' will emerge to take its place is only hinted at in the book's final scene.

As they move into the 'big room' following supper, Isa thinks again about the plot of the play and of her life: 'Love and hate – how they tore her asunder! Surely it was time someone invented a new plot, or that the author came out from the bushes' [252]. Like Eleanor in *The Years*, she sees a pattern in her own life, but cannot locate its author. Isa then recalls for the third time the report she had read in the morning paper of the woman who had been assaulted by some soldiers. 'What then?' she asks herself as she tries to imagine the rest of this story. Her question recalls Eleanor's ' "And now?" ' at the close of *The Years*; again like Eleanor, Isa seems to be interrogating not only this single event, but also the future. As she then looks at Lucy, Bart, and Giles, they become insects 'rolling pebbles of sun-baked earth through the glistening stubble.' Lucy contributes unknowingly to this decreative vision as she reads in her Outline of History that 'England . . . was then a swamp. Thick forests covered the land. On the top of their matted branches birds sang'. These birds may be ancestors of the starlings that Miss La Trobe has heard in the previous scene 'syllabling discordantly life, life, life, . . .' Their 'quivering cacophony' seems to inspire the vision of her next play: ' "I should group them," she murmured, "here." It would be midnight; there would be two figures, half concealed by a rock. The curtain would rise. What would the first words be? The words escaped her' [245–6]. She hears these words as they bubble up out of the mud at the end of the next scene, but we do not. Nor do we hear what Isa and Giles say to each other as they seem to become, in the scene that begins as the book ends, the two figures Miss La Trobe has envisaged: 'Then the curtain rose. They spoke.' As at the close of *The Waves*, the perspective shifts in the final paragraphs to present another time and place, one which fuses the unrecorded past the narrator had earlier imagined being silently sung in the empty dining room with the unacted future. The story of love and hate Isa and Giles are about to enact is a depressingly familiar replay of the old one, but the 'life' that may be born out of their embrace, like the words that will break the silence between them, has at least the potential to become the 're-created world', the new plot Isa has hoped for. 'What then?' we are left like Isa and, it seems like Woolf, to ask.

Conclusion: The novelist must tell a story . . .

The earlier typescript draft of *Between the Acts* contains a passage, linked to the description of the empty dining-room, in which Woolf meditates on the problem of naming 'that which notes that a room is empty.' This observer must have a name, she writes, because 'without a name what can exist?' Yet the names that have been given to 'this haunter and joiner', such as novelist, poet, sculptor, or musician, are, she implies, inadequate.

> This nameless spirit then, who is not 'we' nor 'I,' nor the novelist either; for the novelist, all agree, must tell a story; and there are no stories for this spirit; this spirit is not concerned to follow lovers to the altar, nor to cut chapter from chapter; and write as novelists do 'The End' with a flourish; since there is no end; this being, to reduce it to the shortest and simplest word, was present in the dining-room at Pointz Hall . . .[6]

Although Woolf did not include this passage in *Between the Acts*, she did give this unnamed spirit a voice, not only in the description of the empty dining-room, but also in the recurring intrusions of the gnomic 'third voice' that is reported by the narrator to be saying 'something simple' which we never hear. Miss La Trobe who, like the novelist, cannot escape the necessity of telling a story, seems, like Lily and Bernard before her, to recognize the existence of this other voice. In her desire for words without meaning and for a play that would require no audience, she seeks the anonymity and the freedom from the life in time that this nameless being enjoys. And it may be that her desires are fulfilled, for the scene that begins as the narrative stops has no audience, and the words Isa and Giles speak have no meaning for us. Perhaps the 'true story' that Woolf and her characters have so consistently sought to tell is being told now, we are invited to imagine, 'on the far side of silence'.

6 *Virginia Woolf: 'Pointz Hall'. The Earlier and Later Typescripts of 'Between the Acts'*, ed. Mitchell A. Leaska (New York: University Publications, 1983), p. 62.

Chronological Table[1]

1878   Marriage of Julia Prinsep Jackson Duckworth, a widow with three children (George, Gerald, Stella), to Leslie Stephen, a widower with one child, Laura.

1882   25 January Adeline Virginia Stephen born in London at 22 Hyde Park Gate, third of the Stephens' four children (Vanessa 1879–1961, Thoby 1880–1906, Adrian 1883–1948).

1891   Stephen children begin to issue *The Hyde Park Gate News* (appears weekly until 1895). VW and Vanessa educated at home by their parents and governesses.

1895   Julia Stephen dies (5 May), aged 49. That summer VW has her first breakdown.

1897   VW begins to keep a regular diary; starts lessons again and reads extensively in her father's library. In July, her half-sister Stella Duckworth Hills dies. In November, VW attends Greek and history classes at King's College, London.

1898   VW concludes her diary; attends classes at King's College in Greek with Dr Warr and in Latin with Clara Pater, sister of Walter Pater.

1900   In October VW attends classes at King's College.

1901   VW takes up bookbinding.

---

1 The following chronology is based on Quentin Bell, *Virginia Woolf: A Biography*, 2 vols. (London: Hogarth Press, 1972) and E.L. Bishop, *A Virginia Woolf Chronology* (London: Macmillan, 1988). Although she is Virginia Stephen until her marriage, for the sake of clarity her name will be abbreviated throughout to VW.

1902   VW begins private lessons in Greek with Janet Case. In June Leslie Stephen created KCB in the Coronation Honours and in December is operated on for cancer. Vanessa attends Royal Academy Schools and Thoby and Adrian Trinity College, Cambridge.

1903   VW resumes Greek lessons with Janet Case in October; begins to keep a diary again.

1904   Sir Leslie Stephen dies (22 February), age 71. In May VW's second serious breakdown begins. Spends nearly three months at the home of close friend Violet Dickinson, where she attempts to commit suicide by throwing herself from a window. In October is convalescent and returns to London. Helps F.W. Maitland with his biography of her father and in November begins to send articles to Mrs Lyttleton, editor of the Women's Supplement of the *Guardian*, a weekly newspaper for the clergy. On 14 December her first publication, a review of W.D. Howell's *The Son of Royal Langbrith*, appears in the *Guardian*, followed the next week by 'Haworth, November 1904', an account of her recent visit to the Brontë home. Writes 'literary exercises' and keeps a diary, which includes a record of her first wages for the *Guardian* articles – £2 7s. 6d.

1905   VW 'discharged cured' by her doctor in January. Starts giving classes at Morley College, an evening institute for working women and men, where she teaches until the end of 1907. Continues to keep a diary. In March her long and fruitful relationship with *TLS* begins. Publishes 35 articles and reviews in *TLS*, the *Guardian*, *Academy and Literature*, and *National Review*. In February the 'Bloomsbury Group' begins as Thoby Stephen starts 'Thursday evenings' at 46 Gordon Square, where the Stephens moved following their father's death. Those who attend include Clive Bell, Desmond MacCarthy, Lytton Strachey, Leonard Woolf (hereafter LW), Vanessa, and VW. In October Vanessa starts 'The Friday Club', which is concerned with the fine arts.

1906   VW publishes 21 reviews, mainly in *TLS*, and writes short fiction. In September travels to Italy and Greece with her sister, brothers, and Violet Dickinson (records impressions in a notebook), returning to London in November. On 20 November Thoby Stephen dies of typhoid fever, age 26, and on 22 November Vanessa agrees to marry Clive Bell.

1907   VW publishes nine articles and reviews, continues to keep a diary, writes a comic life of Violet Dickinson ('Friendships

Gallery') and begins her first novel, *The Voyage Out* (called initially *Melymbrosia*). Vanessa and Clive Bell marry. VW and Adrian move to 29 Fitzroy Square, where they resume 'Thursday evenings'. In December VW decides to give up teaching.

1908   VW publishes 19 articles and reviews, completes 100 pages of *VO* by August, takes German lessons, and reads G.E. Moore's *Principia Ethica* (1903). Travels in September to Italy with the Bells and records some of her impressions in a notebook.

1909   In February Clive Bell reads and criticizes seven chapters of *VO*. VW publishes 16 articles and reviews; writes 'Memoirs of a Novelist', hoping Reginald Smith, editor of *Cornhill Magazine*, will publish it as the first in a series of fictional portraits, but he turns it down. In March dines for the first time with Lady Ottoline Morrell, and in April travels with the Bells to Florence, keeping a journal during the trip. Receives proposals of marriage from Lytton Strachey (quickly withdrawn) and Hilton Young (whom she refuses).

1910   In January VW volunteers to work for Women's Suffrage; in February takes part in 'Dreadnought Hoax'. First Post-Impressionist Exhibition ('Manet and the Post-Impressionists'), organized by Roger Fry, opens at Grafton Galleries, London, in November. After undergoing a rest-cure during the summer, resumes work in November on *VO*. Publishes four reviews.

1911   VW publishes two reviews and continues work on *VO*. In late summer begins seeing LW, on leave from Ceylon, frequently. Proposals of marriage from Walter Lamb and Sydney Waterlow, both declined. Starts living at 38 Brunswick Square, London, in November, with Adrian, John Maynard Keynes, Duncan Grant, and after 4 December, LW.

1912   Receives proposal of marriage from LW in January and accepts in May. Becomes ill in February and spends two weeks in nursing home. Completes *VO* in May, begins revising in December. VW and LW marry on 10 August; travel six weeks in Provence, Spain, and Italy. Publishes two reviews.

1913   VW publishes three reviews. Manuscript of *VO* delivered to Gerald Duckworth in March and accepted for publication in April. VW grows increasingly unwell and in July enters nursing home for two weeks; in September attempts suicide by taking overdose of veronal. Under care of LW and nurses.

1914 By January VW able to read and write letters; types a story for Lytton Strachey. Convalesces, travels, visits friends. (4 August Britain declares war on Germany.)

1915 VW begins to write diary in January; Woolfs decide to buy printing press, take Hogarth House, Richmond. Recurrence of mental illness begins in February; taken to nursing home on 25 March while LW moves into Hogarth House. *The Voyage Out* published 26 March and is well received by reviewers. VW brought to Hogarth House in April; four nurses in attendance; gradual improvement begins in June; last nurse leaves in November.

1916 VW recovering, publishes 15 articles and reviews, begins *Night and Day*. Lectures to Richmond Branch of Women's Co-operative Guild, which will hold monthly meetings at Hogarth House for next four years. LW exempted from military service because of trembling hands. Vanessa Bell and Duncan Grant move to Charleston, Sussex. Friendship with Katherine Mansfield begins.

1917 VW publishes 35 articles and reviews, continues writing *ND*. VW and LW buy printing press (replaced in October by larger one) and in July Publication No. 1 of the Hogarth Press appears, *Two Stories* ('Three Jews' by LW and 'The Mark on the Wall' by VW). VW resumes keeping a diary in August. Sets type for K. Mansfield's story *Prelude*. Pays first visit to Garsington Manor, home of Philip and Ottoline Morrell near Oxford.

1918 VW publishes 43 articles and reviews. Finishes *ND* in November; begins printing *Kew Gardens* and writing 'Solid Objects'. In April Harriet Shaw Weaver brings the manuscript of *Ulysses*, hoping Hogarth Press will publish it (it will be published in Paris in 1922). *Prelude* published in July. T.S. Eliot, who will become a lifelong friend, first visits in November. VW visits K. Mansfield often in November and December. (Armistice Day 11 November.)

1919 VW publishes 44 articles and reviews, including 'Modern Novels' (later retitled 'Modern Fiction'). *ND* submitted to Gerald Duckworth in April and published in October to mixed responses. Admired by her friends, although E.M. Forster prefers *VO* and K. Mansfield critical of its traditional method and failure to acknowledge the effects of the war. Ford Madox Ford praises it as 'romance'. Hogarth Press publications include *Kew Gardens*, with two woodcuts by Vanessa Bell, and T.S. Eliot's

Poems. Woolfs buy Monks House, Rodmell, Sussex in July and move there in September; this will be their country home for the rest of their lives.

1920   VW publishes 33 articles and reviews, two stories ('An Unwritten Novel' and 'Solid Objects'); writes stories for *Monday or Tuesday* and in April begins *Jacob's Room*. American editions of *The Voyage Out* (revised) and *Night and Day* published. Memoir Club founded in March (members: Molly and Desmond MacCarthy, VW and LW, Saxon Sydney-Turner, John Maynard Keynes, L. Strachey, Duncan Grant, Vanessa and Clive Bell, E.M. Forster, Sydney Waterlow, R. Fry, David Garnett); VW reads paper in November. Last meeting with K. Mansfield, who is going abroad, in August.

1921   VW publishes 14 articles and reviews; Hogarth Press (VW's British publisher hereafter) publishes *Monday or Tuesday*, a collection of eight stories and sketches, which is praised by friends, most notably R. Fry, L. Strachey, E.M. Forster, and T.S. Eliot, and by reviewers. (*MT* published in US in November by Harcourt Brace.) Studies Russian with S.S. Koteliansky and finishes a draft of *JR* in November. Ill in the summer and unable to write for two months.

1922   VW ill with influenza in January and February; resumes writing *JR* in March, finishes in July, publishes in October. Publishes five reviews. Writing 'Mrs Dalloway in Bond Street', which in October 'branches into a book' (*Mrs Dalloway*). Translating Dostoevsky (with S.S. Koteliansky); begins work on *The Common Reader*. Reads *Ulysses* in book form, judges it a 'misfire' despite Eliot's enthusiasm. In June Eliot dines and reads aloud *The Waste Land*. VW attempts organize Eliot Fund; in December meets Vita Sackville-West, who will become another lifelong friend.

1923   VW publishes 11 articles and reviews, including 'How It Strikes a Contemporary' and the first version of 'Mr Bennett and Mrs Brown', and two stories ('In the Orchard' and 'Mrs Dalloway in Bond Street'). Working on first draft of *Mrs Dalloway* (called at this stage *The Hours*), essays for *The Common Reader*, first version of her play *Freshwater*, and with S.S. Koteliansky, translations of Tolstoy. Sets type for *The Waste Land*, published by Hogarth Press in September. Katherine Mansfield dies 9 January.

1924   VW publishes 36 articles and reviews. Writing *MD* (in March finishes first draft and begins second), *CR* essays, and in

November begins 'The New Dress', first in series of eight stories set at Mrs Dalloway's party. Woolfs move in March from Hogarth House to 52 Tavistock Square, Bloomsbury.

1925 VW publishes *The Common Reader*, *Mrs Dalloway*, and 34 articles and reviews. Writes series of eight stories; begins *To the Lighthouse* in August, stops in September because of illness.

1926 VW resumes writing *TL* in January, finishes first draft in September, and begins revising in October. Publishes 21 articles and reviews and 'A Woman's College from Outside', a story originating in the holograph of *Jacob's Room*. With LW visits Ottoline Morrell, Thomas Hardy, Robert Bridges, V. Sackville-West, among others.

1927 VW publishes *To the Lighthouse* on 5 May (her mother's deathday), 'The New Dress', and 16 articles and reviews. Writes 'Moments of Being: "Slater's Pins Have No Points" '; in October sets aside 'Phases of Fiction' (1929) to begin *Orlando*. Agrees to sponsor and edit Hogarth Living Poets series. Vanessa Bell starts Sunday evening gatherings of Old Bloomsbury. Woolfs buy their first car, a Singer.

1928 VW publishes ' "Slater's Pins Have No Points" ', *Orlando*, and 25 articles and reviews. Finishes first draft of 'Phases of Fiction', begins second; reads two papers at Girton and Newnham colleges, Cambridge, which will become *A Room of One's Own*; records in diary thoughts for next book (*The Waves*). Wins Femina Vie Heureuse prize for *To the Lighthouse*. *Orlando* her best selling book to date. Travels in France with V. Sackville-West.

1929 VW publishes *A Room of One's Own*, 'The Lady in the Looking-Glass: A Reflection', and 14 articles and reviews, including 'Women and Fiction', 'Phases of Fiction', and 'Women and Leisure', a reply to a review of *RO*. Sales of *RO* exceed those of *Orlando*. Writes short fiction, including early draft of 'The Searchlight', and begins first draft of *The Waves* (also called at first *The Moths* or *Moments of Being*).

1930 VW publishes five articles and reviews, finishes first draft of *Waves* and begins second. Friendship with composer Dame Ethel Smyth develops. Woolfs buy new press, old one goes to Sissinghurst Castle, V. Sackville-West's new home.

1931 VW publishes *The Waves* (which outsells previous books), and five articles and reviews. Begins *Flush*, biography of Elizabeth Barrett-Browning's spaniel, sketches 'caricatures', works on essays for second *Common Reader*. Gives speech in January to National Society for Women's Service which will become nucleus of *The Years* (1937) and *Three Guineas* (1938). Sits to Stephen Tomlin for sculptured head.

1932   VW publishes *The Common Reader: Second Series*, and eight articles and reviews, including 'A Letter to a Young Poet'. Writes 'The Shooting Party'; works on *Flush*; in October begins *The Years* (called at this stage *The Pargiters*). Lytton Strachey dies on 20 January.

1933   VW publishes *Flush*, one review, and an article on 'The Novels of Turgenev'. Writing *Years*. Declines offer of honorary doctorate from Manchester University.

1934   VW finishes first draft of *Years* and begins to rewrite. Publishes four articles and reviews. Rewrites *Freshwater*. With LW visits Elizabeth Bowen in Ireland. Roger Fry dies in September; VW asked to write his biography.

1935   VW publishes 'The Captain's Death Bed'. *Freshwater* performed in January in Vanessa Bell's studio. Rewriting *Years* (decides on this title in September) and finishes first revision in December. Writes portions of *Three Guineas*. Reads Roger Fry's letters for biography. Declines to be recommended for Companion of Honour. In May, Woolfs tour Holland, Germany, Italy, and France by car.

1936   VW unwell much of the year, suffering from strain of revising *Years*. Finishes correcting proofs in November and begins writing *Three Guineas*. Reading for *Roger Fry*. Publishes one article, 'Why Art Today Follows Politics' (in the *Daily Worker*), and reads 'Am I a Snob?' to Memoir Club.

1937   *The Years* published; in June heads *New York Herald Tribune* best-seller list for several weeks. VW publishes four articles, including radio broadcast, 'Craftsmanship'. Begins revising short stories for publication in *Harper's Bazaar*; writes and revises *Three Guineas*; reads for *Roger Fry*. Nephew Julian Bell killed driving ambulance in Spain in July.

1938   VW publishes *Three Guineas* to praise of reviewers, criticism of some friends and relations. Publishes two stories ('The Shooting Party' and 'The Duchess and the Jeweller'), two articles, and obituary of Ottoline Morrell, who dies in April. Works on *Roger Fry* and begins *Between the Acts* (called initially *Pointz Hall*). Sells her share of Hogarth Press to John Lehmann.

1939   VW publishes 'Lappin and Lapinova', and four articles and
        reviews. Working on *Roger Fry* and *Between the Acts*. Writes
        another draft of 'The Searchlight', 'Gipsy, the Mongrel', and
        begins her memoir, 'A Sketch of the Past'. Declines offer of
        honorary doctorate from Liverpool University. In January
        with LW visits Sigmund Freud in Hampstead (he gives her a
        narcissus), whose work she will read for the first time later in
        the year. Hogarth Press and Woolf's belongings moved to 37
        Mecklenburgh Square. Travel in France in June. (3 September
        Britain declares war on Germany.)

1940   VW publishes *Roger Fry: A Biography* and nine articles and
        reviews, including 'The Leaning Tower', a paper read in April
        to the Workers' Educational Association in Brighton. Writes
        Between the Acts (which she finishes in November), 'The
        Legacy', further drafts of 'The Searchlight'. Stops writing 'A
        Sketch of the Past' in November; begins 'Anon' and 'The
        Reader', opening chapters of an unfinished history of English
        literature. Declines E.M. Forster's offer to propose her as a
        member of London Library Committee. During Battle of
        Britain Woolf's house in Mecklenburgh Square bombed;
        Hogarth Press moved to Letchworth, books and furniture to
        Monks House.

1941   VW publishes 'Ellen Terry' (earlier rejected, along with 'The
        Legacy', by *Harper's Bazaar*) and 'Mrs Thrale'. Finishes
        revising *Between the Acts* but judges it 'too slight and sketchy'
        to publish. Writes short fiction, including 'The Symbol' and
        'The Watering Place'. Becomes increasingly unwell and fears
        going mad again. On 28 March drowns herself in the River
        Ouse. Her body is found three weeks later and cremated in
        Brighton on 21 April. LW buries her ashes at the foot of a great
        elm tree in the Monks House garden.

Bibliography[1]

The standard bibliography of works by Virginia Woolf is by B.J. Kirkpatrick (Oxford: Clarendon Press, 3rd ed. 1980). Three bibliographies of secondary material direct readers to books and articles written about Woolf's works: Robin Majumdar, *Virginia Woolf: An Annotated Bibliography of Criticism* (New York: Garland Pub., 1976); Thomas Jackson Rice, *Virginia Woolf: A Guide to Research* (New York: Garland Pub., 1984); and Makiki Minow-Pinkney, *An Annotated Critical Bibliography of Virginia Woolf* (Brighton: Harvester Press, 1988).

Quentin Bell's two-volume biography, *Virginia Woolf* Hogarth Press, 1972), may be supplemented by two later biographies which include as well some discussion of her works: *Woman of Letters: A Life of Virginia Woolf* by Phyllis Rose (Oxford University Press, 1978) and *Virginia Woolf: A Writer's Life* by Lyndall Gordon (Oxford University Press, 1984). Quentin Bell's *Bloomsbury* (Weidenfeld & Nicolson, 1968) is an excellent introduction to the social and cultural context in which Woolf lived. A more detailed history of this context can be found in S.P. Rosenbaum's *Victorian Bloomsbury* (Macmillan, 1987) and *Edwardian Bloomsbury* (Macmillan, forthcoming). A subtle and carefully documented analysis of the artistic relationship between Virginia Woolf and her sister is given by Diane Filby Gillespie in *The Sisters' Arts: The Writing and Painting of Virginia Woolf and Vanessa Bell* (Syracuse, NY: Syracuse University Press, 1988).

The amount of criticism written about Woolf's works is vast, and it continues to grow. Some of the initial responses to her works have been collected in *Virginia Woolf: The Critical Heritage*, ed. Robin Majumdar and Allen McLaurin (Routledge & Kegan Paul, 1975).

1 Unless otherwise indicated, place of publication is London.

These early reviews and articles give an historical overview of the progress of Woolf's career and reputation. Book-length studies of her fiction were published during her lifetime, but in general the most suggestive criticism began appearing in the mid 1960s when, for example, Jean Guiget's extensive study, *Virginia Woolf and Her Works* (trans. Jean Stewart) was published by the Hogarth Press (1965). There is room here to name only a few of the many books and articles that have appeared on myriad aspects of Woolf's writings since then. Readers will find, however, that the dialogue among Woolf critics is vigorous and that authors of recent studies will usually direct their readers to other useful books and articles.

The philosophical dimension in Woolf's fiction has interested many of her critics. In 'The Philosophical Realism of Virginia Woolf' (in *English Literature and British Philosophy*, ed. S.P. Rosenbaum [Chicago: University of Chicago Press, 1971], pp. 316–56), S.P. Rosenbaum looks at Woolf's fiction within the context of the writings of the Cambridge philosopher G.E. Moore. In a more recent study, *The Singing of the Real World: The Philosophy of Virginia Woolf's Fiction* (Columbus: Ohio State University Press, 1986), Mark Hussey is concerned not with her debt to any particular philosophical writer, but with the philosophical dimension of Woolf's art.

Many critics have explored the psychological dimension of her work, which can be closely related to the philosophical. Harvena Richter in *Virginia Woolf: The Inward Voyage* (Princeton: Princeton University Press, 1970) and James Naremore in *The World Without a Self: Virginia Woolf and the Novel* (New Haven: Yale University Press, 1973) consider the ways Woolf presents in her fiction the relationship between the external world and the internal one. This subject also figures in Maria DiBattista's wide-ranging book, *Virginia Woolf's Major Novels: The Fables of Anon* (New Haven: Yale University Press, 1980), which places Woolf's fiction within the British comic tradition.

Woolf's representation of the external world is the particular interest of two recent studies. In *The Victorian Heritage of Virginia Woolf: The External World in Her Novels* (Norman, OK: Pilgrim Books, 1987), Janis M. Paul explores the ways in which Woolf's writings bridge the Victorian and the modern period. And in *Virginia Woolf and the Real World* (Berkeley: University of California Press, 1986) Alex Zwerdling shows through a close analysis of Woolf's fiction and her feminist writings how responsive she was to her social and historical context.

This latter aspect of her work has been of special interest to feminist critics, who have written some of the most fruitful recent criticism. Three excellent collections have been edited by Jane Marcus: *New Feminist Essays on Virginia Woolf* (Lincoln: University of Nebraska Press, 1981), *Virginia Woolf: A Feminist Slant* (Lincoln: University of Nebraska Press, 1983), and *Virginia Woolf and Bloomsbury*

(Macmillan, 1987) which, as its title indicates, also contains essays on Woolf's association with the Bloomsbury Group. Rachel Blau DePlessis in *Writing Beyond the Ending: Narrative Strategies of Twentieth-Century Women Writers* (Bloomington: Indiana University Press, 1985), Joanne S. Frye in *Living Stories, Telling Lives: Women and the Novel in Contemporary Experience* (Ann Arbor: University of Michigan Press, 1986) (both of whom discuss Woolf), Ellen Bayuk Rosenman in *The Invisible Presence: Virginia Woolf and the Mother–Daughter Relationship* (Baton Rouge: Louisiana State University Press, 1986), and Makiko Minow-Pinkney in *Virginia Woolf and the Problem of the Subject* (Brighton: Harvester Press, 1987) offer varied and perceptive discussions from a feminist perspective of Woolf's critique of traditional stories and of the narrative strategies used to tell them. Among other things, these studies explore the conjunction in Woolf's works of feminism and modernism.

A recent study that shows how rich an area for discussion Woolf's prose style can be is Kathleen McCluskey's *Reverberations: Sound and Structure in the Novels of Virginia Woolf* (Ann Arbor: UMI, 1986). McCluskey draws on the methods of discourse analysis and structuralism to examine in detail the relationship between the style and the meaning of a selection of Woolf's novels. Other critics, such as Sandra M. Gilbert in 'Woman's Sentence, Man's Sentencing: Linguistic Fantasies in Woolf and Joyce' (*Virginia Woolf and Bloomsbury*), have begun to explore the implications of Woolf's comments in *A Room of One's Own* on the woman writer's need to search for her own style.

Analysts of Woolf's style, like critics of other aspects of her works, sometimes turn to her manuscripts for information. The Monks House Papers at the University of Sussex are available on microfilm (Brighton: Harvester Press). Some of the manuscripts held in the other large Woolf archive, the Berg Collection of the New York Public Library, have been edited and published: '*Melymbrosia': An Early Version of 'The Voyage Out'*, ed. Louise A. DeSalvo (New York: New York Public Library, 1982), *To the Lighthouse: The Original Holograph Draft*, ed. Susan Dick (Toronto: University of Toronto Press, 1982), *The Waves: The Two Holograph Drafts*, ed. J.W. Graham (Toronto: University of Toronto Press, 1976), and Mitchell A. Leaska's editions of '*The Pargiters': The Novel–Essay Portion of 'The Years'* (New York: New York Public Library, 1977) and '*Pointz Hall': The Earlier and Later Typescripts of 'Between the Acts'* (New York: University Publications, 1983). These editions enable critics to consider the evolution of Woolf's texts by tracing the development of particular themes and characters, the refining of image patterns, and so on. The manuscripts, like Brenda R. Silver's helpful description of *Virginia Woolf's Reading Notebooks* (Princeton: Princeton University Press, 1982), the complete editions of Woolf's diaries and letters, the previously unpublished memoirs (*Moments of Being*, ed. Jeanne Schulkind [Hogarth Press, 2nd edn, 1985]), and the complete six-volume edition of her essays currently being edited by Andrew McNeillie and published by Hogarth, enlarge our knowledge of the context in which Woolf lived and wrote and in which her works must now be read. At their best, critical studies of Woolf's extensive writings are doing this, too.

Index